The Maryknoll International Cookbook

Dearest Darlene

Thanks for the
marvelous '75 leave ...
and promoting.

s. Julie

ORBIS BOOKS • 1973 • MARYKNOLL, NEW YORK

The Maryknoll International Cookbook

Complied by
Sister Mary Carol Cannon, M.M.
and
Sister Mary Corde Lorang, M.M.

Editorial consultant
Joseph M. Ferrazza

Contents

vii

Chicken and Other Fowl 83

Fish 97

ix

Stews 113

Rice and Noodles 121

Vegetables 137

Fruits, Desserts, and Candies 153

An Introduction

Food is an even more universal language than music. When it is prepared with love and served with joy, it can be the center of a celebration, whether it be the daily meal of a family or a dinner party for one's friends.

These recipes, from over 40 countries, have been culled with love. Most of them have been given by families overseas to 'foreigners' whom they had learned to love—Maryknoll sisters, brothers and priests who had come to these countries as missioners, doctors, teachers, nurses, carpenters or social workers. Any cook will realize that to 'give away' a favorite recipe, as these families did, is a sign of special trust and affection.

Sometimes, of course, signs of affection can be tendered with love but received with misgivings, as when a first-grader shyly presses a treasured toad into his favorite teacher's palm. A word, then, about these recipes.

Don't be bothered by the strange names—often unappetizing in their sound when not unpronounceable. These are regional recipes from parts of the world most Americans are unfamiliar with. Think how strange "Hamburger steak," "hot dog" or "New England clam chowder" would sound to a native of Guatemala or Thailand (or, for that matter, how odd "Wiener schnitzel" or "minestrone" must have sounded to many of our grandparents, depending on the part of the world *they* came from).

Second, these recipes are practical for anyone beyond the canned-soup and TV-dinner stage who enjoys preparing, serving—and eating—foods a bit beyond the ordinary cookbook or restaurant offerings. The ingredients called for are widely available and even the most exotic-seeming can be obtained with comparatively little trouble: beef hearts can be obtained at your supermarket if you give the meat-manager a few days' notice; a suckling pig for an Hawaiian *luau* may take a day or two longer, depending on your location in the United States.

There is then, literally, a world of cooking for you in the pages of this book, whether you are interested in one recipe, a complete meal from one country or continent, or an international meal with a variety possibly greater than that of the delegates' restaurant at the United Nations headquarters in New York.

A final word, which we could not omit but which any reader may easily skip if so inclined. In almost every religion of which there is record, food and drink have had a meaning for the spirit as well as for the body. Every meal is—or can be—a grateful recognition of the gods—a recognition made most explicit in Judaism through its constantly renewed Passover meal, and in Christianity wherein Passover, the Last Supper and the Eucharist find their echoes in every sharing of food or drink. A slight selection of table prayers is given here to reflect and perhaps heighten that awareness. We hope you will find both prayers and recipes varied enough to suit your needs and even your moods.

"Food, prepared with love and served with joy, can be the center of a celebration." We hope these recipes will help you celebrate with your family and friends—many, many times. And we wish to thank Mr. Charles Flaim, manager of Saga Food Service, for his professional advice.

Sr. Carol Cannon, M.M.
Sr. Mary Corde Lorang, M.M.

Grace Before Meals

Whether we eat or drink, or whatsoever we do, let us do all to the glory of God.

I. COR. X. 31

Out of Thy unmeasured bounty, O Thou lavish Giver of all good, we receive these elements of physical sustenance. May we, through them, partake of the Living Bread which comes down out of Heaven. May we, through them, drink of that Spring which slakes all thirst, that we be nourished to the growth Divine, to the end that our lives may become Thy Life, Thy Life our Lives. In the Name of Him who taught us to give thanks. Amen.

O Thou Who clothest the lilies
And feedest the birds of the sky;
Who leadest the lambs to the pasture
And the hart to the waterside;
Who hast multiplied loaves and fishes,
And converted water into wine,
Do Thou come to our table
As Guest and Giver to dine.

R. EURINGER

God grant that in partaking of this food we may be mindful of those who go hungry, and so strengthen our purpose, that by our daily deeds of service the day may be brought nearer when no man shall want for food or fellowship.

We thank Thee, O Lord, for this good food that You have provided; help us to think of all those children in all countries who this day are hungry and grant that they, too, may have plenty.

S. J. SHAW

We give Thee thanks, our Father, for the holy Resurrection which Thou hast manifested to us through Jesus Thy Son; and even as this bread which is here on this table was formerly scattered abroad, and has been compacted and made one, so may Thy Church be re-united from the ends of the earth for Thy Kingdom, for Thine is the power and glory for ever and ever. Amen.

ATTRIBUTED TO ST. ATHANASIUS

For every cup and plateful
God make us truly grateful.
A. S. F. FISHER

May the grace of love, courage, gaiety, and the quiet mind, which is the grace of the Lord Jesus, be with us now and always.

ROBERT LOUIS STEVENSON

Noisy, vain repetitions are an abomination unto Thee, O God. Make us to pray our prayer with loving heart and hidden words, for Thou will do all that is necessary for our daily needs.

EGYPTIAN c. 900 B. C.

God bless the providers, the dividers, and the devourers.

O God, we have very much . . .
iceboxes, and cars, and automatic toasters,
and our world of things is very great.
Help us not to confuse things with people, because
thou has taught us to use things and to love people
and not the other way around. Amen.

RICHARD WONG—HAWAII

Lord our God,
You have freed your people
from the food of slavery,
and have made them taste
the bread of liberty,
the salt of wisdom,
and the new wine of love.
Bless this meal,
and fill us with your Spirit.

Blessed art Thou, O Lord our God, King of the universe, Who feedest the whole world with Thy goodness, with grace, with loving kindness and tender mercy; Thou givest food to all flesh, for Thy loving kindness endureth forever. Through Thy goodness food has never failed us: O may it not fail us for ever and ever for Thy great Name's sake, since Thou nourishest and sustainest all beings, and doest good unto all, and providest food for all Thy creatures Whom Thou hast created. Blessed art Thou, O Lord, Who givest food unto all.

FROM THE HEBREW

For all the glory of the Way,
For Thy protection night and day;
For roof-tree, fire, and bed and board,
For friends, and home, we thank Thee, Lord.

M. ELIZABETH WORSFOLD

May the blessing of the loaves and fishes which our Lord shared among the multitude, and Grain from the King who made the sharing, be upon us and on our partaking. Amen.

GAELIC GRACE OF THE 6TH CENTURY

For good food and good company, we praise Thee, Lord. Sustain also, we beseech Thee, the needs of others, so that we may always give Thee thanks, through Jesus Christ our Lord. Amen.

FROM THE LATIN

For the farmers who have worked that we may eat,
For those who have bought and sold this food,
For those who have prepared it,
And most of all, for you, Who planned it,
We thank You, Lord.

Feeder and Food to them that love Him, may we recognize Jesus in the beginning and ending of every meal of His bounty, that His grace and blessing may ever "come to pass" to us as He "sits at meat with us."

J. B. OWEN

Praised be my Lord for our mother the earth, which sustains us and keeps us, and brings forth fruits and flowers and many colors, and grass. Praised be my Lord for all those who pardon one another for his love's sake, and who endure weakness and tribulation. . . . Praise ye and bless ye the Lord, and give thanks unto him, and serve him with great humility.

ST. FRANCIS OF ASSISI

Our Father in heaven and here, creator of sun and stars, keeper of homes and children, we thank you for the food which you put into the earth and for the hands which prepared it for us. Help us to look up to thy greatness and to live up to thy goodness. Amen.

RALPH W. SOCKMAN

Father, for our daily food, for the light of Thy truth, for Thy hearing of our prayers, and for every manifestation of Thy Presence, we thank and praise Thee. Amen.

FROM THE CHINESE

Blessed be the hands that work to feed us,
Yellow and black, and brown and white.
Accept our thanks O Lord of Light. Amen.

For the food we are about to eat, Lord Jesus make
us grateful,
Bless all those who helped to grow it, and those
who made it tasteful.

With thankful hearts, O Lord, we ask that we
May never dine without remembering Thee;
And, grateful for our comfortable state,
May leave no Lazarus hungry at the gate.

MAURICE HEALY

Help us, O God, to feed not only upon bread that nourishes bone and sinew but upon the radiance of flowers, and the purity of a selfless act, for we are whole people who must feed on bread, beauty, and compassion. Amen.

RICHARD WONG—HAWAII

Ask for what you want, thank God for what you receive, and don't grumble.

All earth's good gifts to Thee belong;
In Thee our fellowship is strong.
Lord, this our meal together make
Thy Sacrament, for Jesus' sake. Amen.

O God, our heavenly Father, who hast promised to provide, not for our every whim or wish, but for our every need, we thank Thee for these mercies. Grant unto us a due sense of appreciation, for those whose hearts and hands have wrought for us. Help us to share with others, that all Thy children may be strong in body, mind and spirit. Sanctify our fellowship by Thy presence; and may Thy blessing abide in our hearts.

CHARLES D. BRODHEAD

Heavenly Father, you have given us our daily bread. Out of our abundance may we remember those of Your children who cry aloud to You for bread—but have it not.

Thou hast given so much to us, give one thing more; a grateful heart.

Lord we thank Thee for this place in which we dwell; for the love that unites us; for the peace accorded us this day; for the hope with which we expect the morrow; for the health, the work, the food, and the bright skies that make our lives delightful; for our friends in all parts of the earth, and our friendly helpers.

ROBERT LOUIS STEVENSON

Idea Menus from Foreign Lands

AFRICA

African Stew
Page 114

Ugali made with Beans
Page 150

Kisamvu
Page 138

Kachambali
Page 46

Baked Banana Pudding
Page 165

CHILE

Cazuela Chilena
Page 32

Papas Rellenas
Page 79

Porotos Granados
Page 152

Torta Con Pina
Page 154

CHINA

Mock Shark Fin Soup
Page 32

Peking Duck
Page 90

Sweet-Sour Pork
Page 58

Tea Eggs
Page 37

Shrimp and Mushrooms
Page 110

Sesame Seed Leaves
Page 156

GUATEMALA

Bacon Guacamole
Page 15

Avocado Soup
Page 24

Guatemalan Fried Rice
Page 128

Fried Enpanadas
Page 71

Nuégados
Page 166

HAWAII

Pineapple-Bacon Quick Tricks
Page 16

Queen Emma's Avocado Salad
Page 42

Chicken Curry
Page 89

Guava Sherbet   Coffee
Page 161

INDIA

Steamed Rice

Curried Meat with Mango Chutney
Page 70

Grated Coconut and Orange Slices

Sliced Tomatoes

Chopped Salted Cashew Nuts

Chopped or Finely Sliced Onions

Tea

JAPAN

Mandarin Soup
Page 31

Sliced Ginger Root in Vinegar

Teriyaki Meats
Page 66

Green Tea

KOREA

Mantu
Page 27

Noodles with Vinegar-Sesame Sauce
Page 124

K'ong Namul I
Page 53

Fresh Fruit

PHILIPPINES

Chicken with Pork Adobo and Boiled White Rice
Page 87

Squash with Coconut
Page 142

Caramel Custard
Page 157

PERU

Chicken or Beef Broth with Noodles or Rice

Arroz Con Pato A La Peruana
Page 86

Bachelor's Salad
Page 45

Fresh Corn on the Cob

Fresh Fruit

Demitasse Styled Coffee

VIETNAM

Mi Xao Don
Page 133

Salad Greens

Recipes for
Festive Occasions

ANTICUCHOS

PERU

Planning a barbecue? Here's a spicy Peruvian favorite that will have guests coming back for more. Anticuchos, barbecued beef hearts, are as popular in Peru as hot dogs are in the United States. In Peru, they're sold on street corners, railroad stops, at soccer games and outside movie houses. The enticing aroma tickles your nostrils wherever you go. This is one of Sister Carol Cannon's favorites.

2 beef hearts	Small white potatos
4 tsp. cummin	Pepper to taste
2 cups red wine vinegar	Sauce
2 tbs. chopped garlic	1 cup dried chili peppers
4 tsp. salt	2 tbs. olive oil
2 tbs. mashed peppers	2 tbs. achiote seeds
	Salt to taste

Mix the vinegar, cummin, garlic, salt, mashed pepper and ground pepper into a marinade and pour over the beef hearts which have been cut into 1 inch cubes. Cover and refrigerate overnight.

To prepare the barbecueing sauce, remove the seeds from the peppers. Either grind or pound them into a powder, or else soak them and then mash. Next pound or grind the achiote seeds. Next, combine the pulverized peppers, achiote seeds, the oil, salt and some of the marinade from the beef hearts.

To broil, place marinated meat onto skewers and brush with the above sauce. Then broil over charcoal or in an oven broiler. A small potato is placed on the end of the skewer and cooked at the same time. Brush occasionally with the sauce, as needed. About 3 to 4 minutes on each side is usually sufficient.

Serve the anticuchos with *Aji Molido*, which is a special sauce rather like a very hot mustard, a perfect accompaniment for this dish. Serves 8.

CHA GIO

VIETNAM

Sister Moira Riehl sent this recipe from Vietnam where she spent some time in refugee work during the war.

This recipe makes between 52 and 56 fried pork and crab rolls and is delicious for cocktails, hors d'oeuvres or even as a meal in itself. One bite and you'll know why it's one of Sister's best remembered dishes from her stay in Vietnam.

Stuffing
1 4-oz. package bean
  thread
1 medium Chinese yam,
  about 1 pound
5 green onions
1 onion
½ lb. ground pork
Pepper to taste

1 can crab meat, drained
  and flaked
Rolls
Rice paper rounds,
  purchased
1 cup water
1 tsp. caramelized sugar
1 tsp. dark brown sugar

Soak the bean thread in water about 10 minutes. Drain and cut coarsely with shears. Slice the yam paper thin with a vegetable peeler, then cut into fine threads or slivers. Chop both types of onion and mix all ingredients well. Shrimp may be substituted for crab meat, but should be shelled, deveined and chopped before mixing with the other ingredients.

Preparing the rolls

Cut rice paper rounds into half-circles. Mix water and both sugars into a syrup.

Place a half-circle of rice paper on a flat surface and rub gently with the sugar mixture, making sure it does not become too wet. Allow to stand until 3 or 4 are dampened Fold the half-circle in half again. Place about a teaspoon full of the stuffing near the rounded edge in an oblong shape. Fold over the two sides evenly and then roll to form an oblong "package." Roll firm, but not too tight. Set aside, with the loose edge down to help hold it in place. If the edge has hardened a bit, simply moisten it with the syrup. Continue until all rolls are formed.

To cook, pour cooking oil into a heavy frypan to a depth of about 1½ inches. Heat oil on medium heat.

When hot, slip rolls, open side down, into the hot oil. Fry until golden brown. Remove to a wire cake cooler or similar rack to drain.

Serve hot with leaf lettuce, fresh mint leaves, Chinese parsley, thin sliced cucumbers and small individual bowls of Nuoe Mam Sauce (if you can get to a store that sells Oriental foodstuffs).

To eat, wrap the roll in the lettuce leaf along with the mint, Chinese parsley and cucumber, and dip into the sauce.

FIAMBRE

GUATEMALA

This festive Guatemalan dish is customarily served once a year on either November 1st or 2nd. The recipe was sent to us by Sister Benigna Foley.

Legend has it that a hostess had planned a sumptuous dinner for quite a large gathering. She planned the meal herself and made extensive preparations. Then she instructed her maid on just how she wanted it served.

The story goes that the maid's lover called at the back door. Time passed and the guests arrived. At the very last minute the maid realized it was time to serve, panicked, forgot all her instructions and threw all the various foods together on a single large platter.

The meal was a great success, and a disaster became a custom.

The amounts of the various foods should be judged according to the number of guests. The single platter of food, served with rolls and tortillas, makes up the complete meal.

Luncheon tongue, plain
or corned, cut into
squares

Boiled chicken, deboned
and cut into small
pieces

Pork loin, cooked and
cut into small pieces

Beef, corned or plain,
cut into small pieces

Ham, cooked and cut
into small pieces

Sardines or cooked
mackerel, deboned
and cut into small
pieces

Italian style sausages,
cooked (if necessary)
and cut into small
pieces

Frankfurters, if desired

Carrots, potatoes, string
beans, beets, peas,
cabbage, cauliflower,
all cut into small
pieces

Vegetables above should be cut and cooked the previous day. After cooking, cover with the sauce described below and allow to marinate. Keep refrigerated so vegetables will be thoroughly chilled. Before marinating set aside some vegetables for garnishes.

Sauce

2-3 bunches parsley

2-3 bunches green
onions

¼ cup mustard seed

3 chiles morrones
(peppers)

2 oz. capers

2 pieces powdered ginger
root

Dry mustard, to taste

Grind above to a paste. Add vinegar and oil to make a salad dressing. Salt to taste.

Just before serving, mix meats and vegetables together. Add additional vinegar and or oil, as desired. Finally, add the capers.

To serve, place lettuce leaves on one or more platters, as required by the number of guests. Arrange the salad mixture on the platters. Decorate with olives, pieces of cheese, chili pimentos, cocktail onions, sliced hard-boiled eggs, parsley and anchovies. Then sprinkle grated cheese over the whole.

FORTY-NINER CHICKEN ENCHILADAS

MEXICO

Bring out the guitars and the sombreros for this one contributed by Sister Maria Ynez Cavagnaro. A great crowd pleaser for a great crowd.

2⅓ cups whole tomatoes
   mashed
1 cup water
1 tsp. sugar
1 medium sliced onion
1 clove garlic, mashed
1 sliced green pepper,
   cut small (optional)
2-3 tsp. chili powder
2 tbs. olive oil
1 cup raisins
1 tbs. brown sugar

⅔ cup chopped nuts
⅓ square unsweetened
   chocolate
8 black olives
2 tsp. salt
½ cup chopped cooked
   chicken
1½ cups cut up highly
   seasoned sausage,
   cooked but not hard
1¼ cups shredded cheese

Put olive oil in a saucepan. Heat well but do not burn. Add onion and garlic and brown slightly over low fire. Add tomato, water, brown sugar, chocolate, chili powder and 1 tsp. salt. Bring to a boil and simmer covered over a very low fire for about 1 hour. Stir occasionally to prevent sticking. If sauce gets too thick, add a small amount of water. When sauce is done, add raisins, chopped chicken and sausage. Heat thoroughly, but do not overcook.

Wheat tortillas
2 eggs
Milk, diluted 50/50 with
   water
1 tbs. melted shortening

Chopped parsley to
   garnish
Flour, preferably
   unbleached

To each egg add two tablespoons of the milk/water mixture. Add a pinch of salt and a pinch of sugar. Mix well and add enough flour to make a thin batter. Add shortening. Mix well and fry by full tablespoons on an ungreased griddle until bubbly, then turn and fry until done. They should be slightly brown and a bit crisp around the edges. The tortillas should be thin enough to wrap around the filling, but not so thin that they break easily. This may be regulated by adding a bit more liquid or flour, as needed.

When done, pile one atop the other on a warm oven dish, cover with foil and keep warm. Two eggs make between 6 and 9 tortillas.

To serve, place tortilla on a warm platter. Place a generous tablespoon of the filling (or a little more) in the center of the tortilla. Do not have filling too juicy. Add a pinch of grated white cheese, 1 tsp. chopped peanuts and a pitted black olive, then fold one side of the tortilla over the other. Keep tortillas hot in a warm oven.

Just before serving, pour the juice from the sauce over the top and garnish with crumbled cheese, parsley and a few nuts. Serves 20.

SHIN SU LO

KOREA

Truly a royal dish, served at traditional Korean State Dinners. Sister Gilmary Simmons, M.M., M.D., who served as a physician in Korea, says it is one of her favorites. To make this tasty casserole one needs a Shin Su Lo brazier, although an electric skillet or chafing dish can be used effectively. If the dish is prepared for a small group, one brazier within arm's length may be used, with each guest spooning out his portion on rice. Or small braziers for each guest may be used. Sister tells us that the President's wife has been known to use hundreds of such braziers in serving a large Korean State Dinner.

¼ lb. boneless chicken
¼ lb. pork
⅓ lb. round steak,
  sliced thin

⅓ lb. round steak, ground
1½ cups meat stock,
  seasoned with soy
  sauce and pepper

⅔ cup turnips, sliced thin

½ can mushrooms, sliced thin

⅓ cup ginko or English walnuts

¼ cup water chestnuts, cooked

14 dried red dates

3 eggs

½ cup flour

½ tsp. garlic, finely chopped

1½ tbs. soy sauce

2 tsp. finely chopped green onions with tops

2 tsp. white sesame seed, browned and pulverized

½ tsp. sugar

½ cup sesame or salad oil

¼ tsp. black pepper

½ bunch green onions with tops

⅓ bunch watercress

Use only tender portions of watercress. Boil watercress in water until tender, drain and cut into 1½ inch pieces. Dip several pieces in a batter made of eggs and ½ cup flour. Fry in a small amount of oil until golden brown. Remove and cut into diamonds an inch across.

Cut pork into thin slices, dip in egg batter, fry and cut in same manner.

Season ground meat with half the garlic, soy sauce, chopped onions, sesame seed, sugar, pepper and 1 tsp. sesame oil. Form into flat cakes the size of a half-dollar and a few balls 1 inch in diameter. Dip cakes in egg batter and fry in oil. Mix remaining garlic, soy sauce, sesame seed, sugar, pepper and 2 tsp. oil with the sliced round steak.

Soak dried dates in water for about 1 hour, drain and cut into thin slices. Mix with sliced mushrooms.

Beat the yolk of 1 egg slightly and fry in a very thin layer in a slightly oiled frypan. Fry egg white in the same manner. Remove from pan and cut fried egg into diamonds 1 inch across.

Arrange ingredients in the Shin Su Lo brazier with the raw meat on the bottom and the other ingredients in layers. Garnish with diamonds of egg, green onions and meat balls.

Pour hot soup over mixture in brazier until ⅔ full. Cover and fill center of brazier with several pieces of burning charcoal. (Charcoal may be heated on the range and transferred to the brazier after it begins to burn.)

Cook 10 minutes and serve hot. After serving, brazier may be refilled if desired. Served over hot boiled rice.

LUAU PIG

HAWAII

If you're thinking of entertaining Hawaiian-style, then music, soft lights and plenty of flowers are a must. Lei-stringing is a good way to start the party off. Give each guest a supply of flowers, a large needle and about a yard of heavy thread. Try crepe paper if flowers aren't available.

Have your guests dress informally: slacks and brightly colored shirts for the men; flowered muumuus or holomuus for the ladies.

Decorate your table with greens. Replace your tablecloth with large leaves such as ferns (or cut paper "leaves" from green construction paper if live greens are not available). Make your centerpiece from fruits such as pineapple, coconut, bananas, avocados, papayas and mangos, which will also become part of the dessert. Finally, scatter individual blossoms over the entire table and place a blossom at each guest's place.

Finally, the food. For a truly memorable luau, try this authentic Hawaiian recipe for suckling pig, sent to us by Sister Joan Uhlen.

1 suckling pig, 10 to 12 lbs.	Corn husks
1 can condensed milk	Salt and pepper to taste
¼ lb. butter	2 lbs. spinach, cooked
	3 medium onions, sliced

Choose a tender suckling pig, clean well and hang overnight in a cool place.

In a small saucepan, mix condensed milk, butter, salt and pepper, and bring to a boil. Pour this mixture into pig.

Drain all water from cooked spinach. Mix with sliced onions and stuff pig while spinach mixture is hot.

After pig is stuffed, season the outside by rubbing with salt and pepper mixture. Then wrap entire pig with corn husks and place in a pan in which a small amount of water has been added.

Preheat oven for about 15 minutes, then lower oven temperature to about 350°F. Bake pig about 8 to 10 hours depending upon its size.

When cooked, remove corn husks. If it needs further browning, continue baking without the corn husks until pig is golden brown.

Luau Pig is an excellent substitute for Kalua Pig, which is cooked under the ground at Hawaiian luaus.

To give your luau an authentic island flavor, set a small dish of condiments at each place setting. Use chopped nuts, chili peppers, green onions, salted dried fish and rock salt.

CHAWAN MUSHI

JAPAN

"A dish for a feast day," wrote Sister Marie Elise Bua-mann when she sent us this tasty recipe for steamed egg cups. Miyagima Akemi, a friend of Sister, prepares this tasty traditional Japanese dish when she knows the Sisters are coming for lunch. Try it the next time you entertain special friends at lunch time.

1 piece fish fillet, grated	*Small bundle of spinach*
1 sheet or package	*4 large mushrooms*
* Japanese sea weed*	*2-3 pieces lotus root per*
1 cup water	* cup (may be omitted)*
½ lb. cooked chicken	*3 eggs*
2-3 dried bread sticks	*Salt*
* (hara kiri fu)*	*Pepper*

Prepare a broth from the grated fish fillet, sea weed and water.

Set up 4 custard cups. Fill each ¼ full with the broth.

Dice the chicken into small pieces, chop the spinach and slice the mushrooms in thirds. Break the dried bread sticks into small pieces. Mix together and divide the ingredients into the 4 egg cups. Add the lotus root.

Add salt and pepper to eggs and beat well. Divide beaten egg mixture and pour over the other ingredients.

Cover each cup with aluminum foil. Set up a wire rack inside a large covered kettle into which about ½ inch of water has been simmering. Set egg cups onto rack, cover kettle and steam for about 17 minutes. Serve hot, one cup for each guest.

MANCHURIAN FIRE KETTLE

CHINA

Here's an exciting blend of tastes and textures which is ideal to spring on your guests as a late evening supper or after a casual gathering. This recipe, contributed by Sister Mary deLellis McKenna, is especially satisfying on a cold winter evening.

Stock soup, about 1 cup
Boiled rice, 8 cups

1 saucerful of each
of the following:
Slivered cooked pork
  tenderloin
Chopped onions
Sesame oil
Raw celery, washed
  and finely cut
Boiled chicken, cubed
Soaked Chinese
  noodles

Chinese cabbage finely
  sliced
Raw spinach, washed
  thoroughly
Small fried meatballs
Eggs, fried in thin
  sheets then cut into
  narrow strips

Add to taste:
Ginger root, finely
  chopped
Soya sauce
Vinegar

Prepare rice ahead of time and keep warm and moist in a covered pot.

To prepare use a large kettle, preferably iron. Heat the kettle and add the pork tenderloin which has been previously fried for about 5 minutes. Add all other ingredients, a little at a time, and mix well. Add soup stock as needed to keep the mixture moist but not wet. Continue until all ingredients have been added.

Finally, add ginger root, soya sauce and vinegar to taste.

To serve, provide each guest with an individual bowl of rice and permit each to ladle out as much of the hot fire kettle mixture into his bowl as he likes.

Serve with tea and candied fruits. Serves 6.

Appetizers and Snacks

AVOCADO COCKTAIL

GUATEMALA

Sister Mary Benigna Foley, serving in Guatemala for a good many years as a professional bookkeeper, has many other interests as well. Her keen concern about the nutrition of people in that area and about the food value of native plants, fruits and meats has given her a wide knowledge of foods and an interesting collection of recipes. Here is one of them.

2 medium avocados	2 tsp. minced celery
½ cup tomato catsup	6 drops Tobasco sauce
¼ cup lemon juice	Salt to taste
2 tsp. minced onions	Black pepper to taste

Chill avocados. Peel and cut into thin slices.

Mix catsup, lemon juice, onion, celery, Tobasco and seasoning.

Arrange slices of avocado in chilled cocktail glasses and pour sauce over them. Serve very cold. Serves 4.

EGG APPETIZER

COLOMBIA

4 hard-boiled eggs, chopped	3 tbs. chopped parsley
	2 tbs. lemon juice
2 chopped avocados	1½ tsp. salt
1 chopped onion	
¼ teaspoon ground chili pepper	

Combine all ingredients and mix until well blended and smooth. Chill.

Serve as hors d'oeuvres on lettuce, melba rounds or toast. Serves 6.

BACON GUACAMOLE

GUATEMALA

1 cup mashed avocado	1 tsp. salt
½ cup mayonnaise	¼ tsp. chili powder
2 tbs. lemon juice	Dash cayenne pepper
¼ cup chopped stuffed olives	4 slices crisp-cooked bacon, crumbled
1 tbs. grated onion	

Mix avocado, mayonnaise, lemon juice, olives, onion and seasoning and chill.

Just before serving, stir in bacon and garnish with parsley. Serves 4.

SWEETENED COCONUT CHIPS

PHILIPPINES

Slice coconut meat thin on a mechanical kitchen meat slicer. (A potato peeler may be used.) Mix slices with sugar and a small amount of honey. Heat over a low fire, stirring constantly until the coconut slices are evenly, lightly coated with the mixture. Toast in an oven at about 200°F until chips are golden brown. Chips can be vacuum sealed until ready to use, if desired. Use as a snack.

CHEESE BALLS INDIENNE

GUATEMALA

½ lb. grated cheddar cheese	2 tbs. finely chopped chutney
1 tsp. curry powder	

Mix all ingredients together. Form with fingers into very small balls. Serve on toothpicks.

SALTED COCONUT CHIPS

PHILIPPINES

Pared coconut meat is sliced thin with a mechanical kitchen meat slicer. (A potato peeler may be used.) Mix slices with salt, lactose and dextrose and heat over a low fire with constant stirring until slices are evenly dried. The dried chips are toasted in an oven with the temperature at about 200°F until the chips are golden brown. Use as a snack.

FRUIT COCKTAIL

PHILIPPINES

3 cups ripe papaya,
  diced
3 cups pineapple,
  diced

3 tbs. kalamansi
  (lime) juice
4 tbs. sugar

Mix the ingredients and chill for ½ hour before serving. Serves 12.

PINEAPPLE QUICK TRICKS

HAWAII

These tasty little recipes for pineapple come to us from Sister Joan Uhlen. Note the wide range of tastes and textures you can get with this versatile fruit.

1. Mix cream cheese with the syrup drained from a can of crushed pineapple. Spread cheese on crackers, surround with anchovy fillets and top with the drained crushed pineapple.
2. Serve pineapple chunks on toothpicks along with small bowls of grated cheddar cheese and shredded coconut. Dip a chunk first in the cheese, then in the coconut.
3. Wrap pineapple chunks with bacon, fasten with a colored toothpick and broil. Serve crisp and hot.

GUACAMOLE

GUATEMALA

The girls at Monte Maria in Guatemala City insist that a fiesta is not complete without this dish. Sister Margaret James Roe says that it is also delicious and peppy when used as a dip.

2 medium onions
1 clove garlic
4 medium tomatoes
2 small hot chili
  peppers

4 medium avocados
1 tsp. lime juice
Salt and pepper to
  taste

Grind the onions, garlic, tomatoes and chili peppers together. Mash the avocados with the lime juice added. Combine the onion mixture and mix well. Add salt and pepper to taste. Mix well and chill.

Serve in the avocado shells or in dip dishes. Serves 6.

GUACAMOLE

MEXICO

Here's another recipe for this famous Latin American dish, this time as it is prepared in Mexico.

1½ cups peeled
  tomatoes, cubed
½ cup green peppers
  cubed
½ cup diced onions
2 tbs. lemon juice

¼ tsp. mustard powder
Dash of Tobasco
½ tsp. Worchestershire
  sauce
1 avocado, peeled and
  cubed

Mix the ingredients in the above order. Mash by hand, blending well, or use an electric mixer. Chill.

In Mexico, Guacamole is served as an appetizer or as an accompaniment to a green salad. Serves 4 to 6.

SALMON APPETIZER

HAWAII

1 lb. smoked salmon
12 scallions
¼ cup ice water

½ tsp. salt
4 peeled tomatoes,
  chopped

Soak salmon for 3 hours in cold water, changing water frequently. Drain salmon well, removing skin and small bones. Shred salmon.

Shred scallions until they are of paste-like consistency. Add ice water and salt.

Combine salmon and tomatoes and mash with fork until smooth. Add scallion paste and mix well. Chill and serve as hors d'oeuvres. Serves 6.

Soups

PEANUT SOUP

UGANDA

2 tbs. cornstarch
3 cups milk
3 cups chicken stock
Pinch cayenne pepper

2 cups ground peanuts
2 tbs. grated onions
2 tsp. salt

In a deep saucepan, place cornstarch and slowly add milk. Stir until smooth. Add remaining ingredients, stirring constantly. Bring quickly to a boil. Continue cooking 5 minutes over medium heat. Beat for 1 minute with a rotary beater. Strain and serve hot. Serves 6.

LENTIL SOUP

SAUDI ARABIA

½ cup lentils
2 cups coarsely chopped
  onions
2 tsp. salt
Juice of ½ lemon

8 cups water
1 cup chopped Swiss
  chard or spinach
2 tbs. olive oil

Wash lentils thoroughly and put into salted water in a large soup kettle. Add onions and mix. Cook over medium heat for 1 hour, or until lentils are tender. Add Swiss chard or spinach, olive oil and lemon juice. Serves 6–8.

For variety, this recipe can be made with lamb. Add 1 lb. cubed lean lamb to the lentils and simmer over a medium heat. Stir thoroughly before serving. Serves 8.

MINALI KUK

KOREA

½ lb. lean beef or pork
3 cups water

1 tsp. soy sauce
1½ tsp. salt

¼ cup finely sliced onion
1 tbs. finely sliced fresh
  or preserved ginger root

1 small clove garlic
1 lb. watercress

Cut meat into slices about ½ inch wide, 2 inches long and ¼ inch thick. Place into a deep saucepan. Add water, soy sauce, salt, onion, ginger and garlic. Simmer for 1 hour.

Wash watercress thoroughly. Discard tough watercress stems. Cut into 2 inch lengths and add to soup. Simmer for 15 minutes longer and serve. Serves 6.

HOH-TAY TANG

CHINA

½ lb. sliced ham
6 cups cold water

1 tsp. salt
1 Chinese cabbage (1 lb.)

Cut ham into ½ inch cubes after removing rind and bone. Put in deep kettle with bone. Add water and salt. Cover kettle, turn heat on high and bring to a rolling boil. Then turn down heat and simmer for 20 minutes.

While simmering, separate and wash cabbage. Lay leaves together and cut into narrow strips. Add to broth, heat to boiling and simmer 10 minutes.

Serve as quickly as possible as soup will turn slightly bitter if allowed to stand too long. Serves 6–8.

SHRIMP CHOWDER

PERU

2 tbs. olive oil
1 clove garlic, crushed
1 medium onion, minced
1 large tomato, chopped
4 cups boiling water
1 cup kernelled corn

¼ cup peas
3 medium potatoes, diced
Chopped parsley
2 tbs. uncooked rice
1 lb. fresh shrimp, cleaned,
  shelled and deveined

Pinch of oregano   *Salt and pepper to taste*
4 slices any fried white   *1 can evaporated milk*
* fish*

Heat the oil in a deep saucepan. Add garlic, onion and tomato and fry for several minutes. Add water, corn, peas, potatoes, rice and bring to a boil. Boil about 10 minutes, or until potatoes are cooked. Lower heat, add shrimp, oregano, salt and pepper and simmer until shrimp are cooked. Remove from heat.

Before serving, reheat soup and add evaporated milk, being careful not to boil or cook too hard as milk may curdle. Add the white fish and sprinkle with parsley. Serves 4–6.

PAICH'U KUK

KOREA

This is a version of Minali Kuk which uses white mustard cabbage in place of watercress.

Prepare soup stock as directed on pages 20-21.
Wash the white mustard cabbage thoroughly. Discard the tough cabbage stems. Cut into 2 inch lengths and add to soup about 15 minutes before soup is done. Serves 6.

EGG SOUP

CHINA

4 cups chicken   *2 tsp. soy sauce*
* consomme*   *2 scallions*
2 eggs

Bring consomme to a boil and dribble in eggs after they have been well stirred. Add soy sauce. (If domestic soy sauce is used, add slowly and taste frequently since it is more concentrated and salty than the Chinese variety.) Salt to taste. Thinly slice the scallions and float on top of the soup. Serves 4–6.

POTATO PUREE

COLOMBIA

Chicken, 1 piece of white
  meat per person
1½ qts. water
1 finely chopped onion
4-5 sprigs parsley,
  minced
Parsley for garnishing

Rosemary leaves
  (optional)
Salt and pepper to taste
1 large baking potato,
  diced
4 medium boiling
  potatoes, diced

Place washed chicken in a soup pot, cover with water
and add onion, parsley, rosemary, salt and pepper. Simmer
until chicken is tender.

After first half hour, add diced baking potato so that
it will disintegrate and give body to the soup.

Then, 15 minutes before serving, add remainder of diced
potatoes. Cook until tender, but not soft. Serves 6.

MUSHROOM SOUP

CHINA

1 quart water
½ lb. beef, sliced thin
⅛ cup mushrooms,
  sliced thin
Pinch of ground ginger
⅛ cup water chestnuts,
  sliced thin

⅛ cup sliced bamboo
  shoots
Salt, pepper and soy
  sauce to taste

Fry sliced beef and ginger in the greased bottom of a
large soup pot. Add 4 quarts of water and bring to a boil.
Continue simmering until liquid has boiled down to half
its original amount.

Strain soup and discard meat. Return to pot. Add mushrooms, water chestnuts and bamboo shoots, and bring to
a boil. Add salt and pepper. Cover and simmer for 10
more minutes. Add soy sauce before serving. Serves 6.

KUKSU KUK

KOREA

¾ lbs. beef shin	¼ tsp. mashed fresh or
¼ lb. lean pork	dried ginger root
6 cups water	1 tbs. soy sauce
1 tsp. salt	¼ lb. noodles

Wipe meat with damp cloth and cut into 2 inch cubes. Place meat into a soup kettle. Add water, ginger root and salt and allow to simmer for 3 hours.

Minutes before serving, add noodles and bring to a boil. Cook until tender. Just before serving, add soy sauce. Serves 6.

AVOCADO SOUP

GUATEMALA

2 tbs. butter	2 cups water
1 tbs. flour	1 bay leaf
1 chopped onion	1 cup mashed avocado
½ cup celery, cut very	1 cup milk
fine	Salt and pepper to taste

Brown onion and flour in butter. Add celery, water, bay leaf, salt, pepper and milk. Simmer until celery is tender. Add avocado and cook 5 minutes. Serve hot. Whipped cream may be stirred in just before serving. Serves 2.

PANCIT MOLO

PHILIPPINES

This delicious, rich and hearty soup made with filled dumplings comes to us from Sister Rita Gregory in the Philippines. It is a "must" at a Filipino banquet. It also makes a tasty one-dish meal when served with a salad and fruit.

½ cup ground pork
¼ cup flaked boiled
  chicken
1 egg
1½ tbs. chopped green
  onions

⅛ cup water chestnuts
¼ cup boiled sliced
  shrimp, shelled and
  deveined
⅛ clove garlic, chopped
Salt and pepper to taste

Combine all ingredients. Divide into 2 parts. Set aside one-half for use with the broth. Wrap the other half in egg noodle wrappers, as below.

Wrappers

1 cup flour
Pinch of salt

2 egg yolks
1 oz. water

Sift together flour and salt. Add egg yolks and knead with fingers. Add water and work dough until it becomes smooth and fine. Roll out on a floured board to a thin sheet about the thickness of paper. Cut into triangular pieces about 3 inches long.

Broth

10 cups chicken broth
¼ clove garlic, chopped
1 oz. butter

5 chopped green onions
Salt and pepper to taste

Saute garlic and onions in the bottom of a large soup kettle. When lightly browned, add that half of the meat mixture which was set aside for use in the broth. Saute together 5 minutes. Add chicken broth and bring to a boil.

Drop wrapped dumplings into boiling broth, cover and let boil for about 15 minutes. Serves 10.

MEAT GARNISH FOR SOUP

KOREA

This and the next recipe for Egg Garnish were sent to us from Korea by Sister Mary Gabriella Mulherin.

½ lb. lean beef
¼ cup onion, finely
  chopped
1⅓ tbs. soy sauce
½ tsp. sugar

2 tsp. white sesame seed,
  browned and pulverized
½ tsp. garlic, finely chopped
2 tsp. sesame or salad oil
2 tbs. finely chopped green
  onion with tops

Combine all ingredients except the green onion. Fry in a hot oiled pan. When meat is cooked, add green onion and mix well. Use 2 tbs. of this mixture for each serving of soup.

EGG GARNISH FOR SOUP

KOREA

2 eggs

½ tsp. peanut or salad oil

Separate yolks from egg whites, saving both. Beat egg yolks slightly. Pour into a slightly oiled frypan, make a very thin layer and fry until firm.

Fry slightly beaten egg whites in the same manner.

Slice fried egg pancakes into as narrow strips as possible. Add as desired to each serving of soup.

GUATEMALAN SOUP

5 whole black pepper-
  corns
5 cummins
1 piece clove
6 tomatoes

6 raw mil tomatoes
  (husk tomatoes)
Coriander, well ground
1 cup rice
3 cups meat broth

Soak rice in enough water to cover. After rice has absorbed the water and softened, drain.

Combine all ingredients and grind well. Add meat soup stock as desired and mix well.

Simmer until all ingredients are cooked. Serve hot. Serves 4.

MANTU

KOREA

Filling for dumplings

1 block tofu (soybean
  curd) or 1½ cups
  cottage cheese
½ lb. lean pork
½ lb. celery cabbage or
  white mustard cabbage
3 tbs. sesame or salad
  oil
¼ cup white sesame
  seed, browned and
  pulverized

1 tsp. sugar
¼ cup soy sauce
2 cups bean sprouts
½ tsp. finely chopped
  garlic
2 tbs. finely chopped
  green onions with tops
½ tsp. salt
Pepper to taste

Parboil beef, pork, cabbage and bean sprouts separately until they are cooked through. Drain and chop these ingredients finely. Squeeze out the excess liquid from the cabbage, bean sprouts and tofu (or cottage cheese). Mix all ingredients thoroughly.

Dumplings

3 cups flour
Water
1 egg

½ tsp. salt
1 tbs. sesame or salad
  oil

Combine flour, egg, salt and oil. Add sufficient water to make a dough. Knead slightly and roll out to a thickness of ⅛ inch on a slightly floured board. Cut circles of dough 3 inches in diameter. Place 2 tbs. of the filling in the center of the circle, fold over and press the edges of the dough together, forming a half-circle.

Soup stock

5½ cups meat broth
2 tbs. soy sauce

1 tsp. salt

Add seasonings to the meat broth and bring to a boil.

Drop the mantu dumplings into the soup and cook for 10 minutes or until the dumplings come to the surface.

Frequently the mantu is cooked in boiling salted water and then served with hot soup. Serve right from the heat. Allow 3 or 4 dumplings for each serving. Garnish with strips of green onion, toasted black seaweed and narrow strips of fried egg yolk and egg white. Rice may be served with the soup, if desired. Serves 6.

CHICKEN SOUP

KOREA

2 tbs. vegetable oil	Dash of black pepper
1 chicken (3 lbs.)	12 cups water
5 tbs. soy sauce	1 tsp. salt
1 scallion, chopped	1 egg
1 clove garlic, chopped	

Cut chicken from the bone and cut into 1 inch pieces. Set aside.

Make the chicken stock by simmering the chicken bones in 12 cups water for about 7 hours.

Place chicken pieces into a bowl. Add soy sauce, chopped scallion, garlic and black pepper. Mix well.

Heat oil in a large heavy skillet. Add chicken mixture and fry until chicken is well seared. Add broth from chicken bones and enough water to make 8 cups. Cook until chicken is tender.

To prepare egg, separate the yolk and white. Beat each slightly with a fork. Cook by circling a small amount of egg yolk over the bottom of a heated oiled skillet, making a round, very thin "pancake." When firm, turn and cook the other side. Repeat with egg whites. Roll each "pancake" separately into a long tube shape and shred crosswise into very fine strips.

To serve, ladle broth into individual bowls, season with salt and decorate each bowl of soup with the shredded egg. Serves 6.

BEAN SOUP

AFRICA

Sister Patricia Hafey sent this recipe to us from Africa where she has been working in Mwanza. It illustrates the strong Indian cultural influence.

1 cup dried beans	*1 green pepper*
2 cups chopped onions	*1 tbs. curry powder*
2 cups tomatoes	*Grated coconut and milk*
Salt and pepper to taste	

Presoak beans, if necessary, and cook along with the tomatoes and pepper until beans are soft. When cooked, put through a sieve. Return the soup to the fire and add the onion and continue cooking. Let the grated coconut stand in 1 cup of coconut milk, then strain and add the liquid to the soup. Cook over a slow fire until it has thickened, adding the seasonings during the last few minutes of cooking.

PERUVIAN SOUP

4 tbs. shortening	*¼ tsp. marjoram*
3 minced medium onions	*1½ tsp. salt*
2 tbs. flour	*Dash of black pepper*
3 cups meat stock (or water)	*3 cups milk, scalded*
4 medium potatoes, peeled and cubed	*½ cup cooked peas*
⅛ tsp. saffron	*3 eggs*
	¼ lb. cream cheese
	1 avocado

In a deep saucepan, melt the shortening and add the onions. Saute for 10 minutes. Add flour and mix until smooth. Add meat stock slowly and allow to come to a boil. Add the potatoes, saffron, marjoram, salt and pepper. Cook over low heat for 20 minutes. Add milk and peas and cook 5 minutes longer.

In a small bowl, soften the cream cheese and blend in the eggs. Gradually pour in 2 cups of the hot potato soup, stirring constantly, then add all the contents of the bowl to the soup in the saucepan. Stir continually for a few minutes until both mixtures are completely blended.

To serve, peel and slice the avocado. Place a few slices into each serving dish and pour the hot soup over it. Should be eaten piping hot. Serves 6.

MEAT BALL SOUP

COSTA RICA

1½ lbs. ground beef	*1 tsp. salt*
2 eggs	*¼ tsp. pepper*
2 finely chopped onions	*Corn meal or flour*
⅛ tsp. marjoram	*2 quarts beef broth*

In a bowl, mix meat, eggs, onions and seasoning. Shape into small balls and roll in corn meal or flour.

Heat broth to a boil in a large soup pot and add the meat balls. Simmer until meat is cooked. Serves 6–8.

P'A KUK

KOREA

3 cups green onions, sliced in 2 inch lengths with tops	*1 tbs. white sesame seeds, browned and pulverized*
⅓ lb. lean beef or ¾ lb. short ribs	*6 cups water*
3½ tbs. soy sauce	*Dash of black pepper*
	¾ tsp. salt

Any lean cut of beef will do. Wipe the meat with a damp cloth and place in a deep soup pot. Add water, soy sauce, sesame seed and salt. Simmer for 1½ hours. Add green onions and cook for 10 minutes longer. Sprinkle with black pepper and serve hot with rice.

If desired, an egg may be beaten into the soup just before serving. Serves 6.

MANDARIN SOUP

JAPAN

Sister Mary Gemma Shea, who contributed this recipe, has been in Japan most of the time since she came to Maryknoll in the very early days. She has become not only a master of the Japanese language but also an expert in Japanese cooking. She tells us that at any banquet in Japan, the soup course is indispensable. Any royal meal would be proud to include this savory dish.

½ lb. lean pork, cut in strips	*2 tbs. cornstarch*
1 tbs. vegetable oil	*2 tbs. soy sauce*
⅓ cup diced carrots	*Salt and pepper to taste*
⅓ cup celery	*¾ cup raw spinach, finely chopped*
⅓ cup onion	*1 large egg, beaten well*
6–8 cups boullion	

Saute meat in oil. Add vegetables and saute for 5 minutes. Add to broth. Add cornstarch mixed with soy sauce, salt and pepper.

Simmer 20 minutes. Before serving, add chopped spinach and egg to boiling soup, stirring well with a fork or whisk. Serves 12.

CARBONADA

CHILE

1 lb. beef or lamb, cut in chunks	*1 cup rice*
½ chopped onion	*Celery and string beans chopped fine, as desired*
Potatoes and carrots, as desired	*Small amount of lard or cooking oil*
3 qts. boiling water	

Brown meat and onions in oil. Put into a large pot of boiling water. Cook until the meat is tender. Add other ingredients and simmer for about 1 hour. Season to taste. Serves 4–6.

MOCK SHARK FIN SOUP

CHINA

Betty Chien, who contributed this recipe, quickly admits that one can no longer buy shark's fins. The soup is delicious, even without the white fin muscles.

2 quarts of a rich chicken broth	4 eggs, well beaten ½ tbs. vegetable oil
Breast of 1 chicken, shredded	

Begin with the rich chicken broth. Add the shredded breast of one chicken.

Heat oil in a frypan. Fry several tablespoons at a time into a thin sheet or "pancake." When cooked, cut the egg pancakes into noodle-like strips. Add to the soup just before serving. Add shredded ham to taste. Serves 8.

CAZUELA CHILENA

CHILE

Sister Genevieve Reinhardt contributed this recipe and tells us it is particularly good in cold weather—for which Chile is famous.

Beef, lamb or chicken with some bone	1 tsp. red pepper
Small whole potatoes	4 quarts water
¼ cup rice or noodles	Pieces of yellow pumpkin squash, if desired
Onions and parsley to taste	

Cut meat into chunks and brown in a large soup kettle. Add the water to the kettle. Add the rest of the ingredients and cook over the low heat until all the meat and vegetables are tender. If desired, the vegetables can be added later so as to retain their individuality.

Egg and Cheese Dishes

CORN MEAL SOUFFLE

GUATEMALA

⅓ cup yellow or white
  corn meal
2 cups milk
1 tbs. butter
3 tbs. grated cheese

1 tsp. salt
¼ tsp. paprika
Pinch cayenne pepper
3 eggs, separated

In a saucepan, heat milk to boiling. Stir in corn meal and butter. Reduce heat and stir in the cheese. Cook to the consistency of mush. Season with spices and egg yolks. Cook and stir for 1 minute longer to permit yolks to thicken. Cool.

Beat egg whites until stiff and then fold into corn mixture. Bake in ungreased baking dish 25 minutes at 350°F until slightly crusty. Serves 6.

EGG CURRY

CEYLON

1 cup dried lentils
3 tbs. butter
2 sliced onions
6 hard-boiled eggs, sliced

1 tbs. curry powder
¾ cup water
1 tsp. salt

Wash lentils and soak them overnight in cold water. Drain well.

Melt butter in saucepan. Add onions and curry powder and saute for 10 minutes, stirring frequently. Add water and lentils. Cover and cook for 45 minutes over low heat. Add salt and sliced eggs. Mix gently and cook for 5 minutes. Serve immediately. Serves 6.

GUATEMALAN CHEESE TORTILLAS

½ can tomato paste

½ tsp. garlic salt

Oregano to taste
3 dozen small toasted
    tortillas

2 oz. cheddar or
    mozzarella cheese
2 oz. salami or pepperoni

Combine tomato paste, garlic salt and oregano. Cut cheese and salami into tiny cubes. Spoon small amounts of tomato mixture on toasted tortillas. Top with cheese and meat cubes. Garnish with oregano.

Bake at 400°F for 3–5 minutes, or until cheese melts. Serve piping hot.

STRING BEAN OMELET

CHILE

6 eggs, separated
½ tbs. flour
½ cup milk
1 tbs. onions, cut fine

½ tbs. lard or salad oil
1 lb. chopped cooked
    string beans
Salt and pepper to taste

Beat egg yolks and whites separately.

Make a white sauce with milk, flour and oil. Add beaten egg yolks slowly. Fold in the beaten egg whites. Gently fold in the other ingredients, except the vegetables. Pour egg mixture into heated greased frypan and place the heated vegetables on top. Brown over a low heat and turn once to brown the other side. Serve immediately. Serves 4–6.

CHILAQUILA

GUATEMALA

4 oz. fresh or cream
    cheese
1 large onion, finely
    chopped
1 tomato, finely chopped

2 eggs, separated
1 tbs. flour
Salt to taste
8 tortillas

Mix cheese, onion and tomato. Place inside tortillas. Fold in half.

Beat egg whites until stiff. Add yolks, flour and salt.
Heat salad oil in a skillet. Dip tortillas in the egg mixture
and fry until golden brown.

Serve hot, with or without tomato sauce. Serves 4.

STEAMED EGG

CHINA

6 eggs
½ cup cooked shrimp or
    meat
¼ cup halved peanuts

Salt to taste
1 tsp. soy sauce
2 tbs. chopped onion

Beat eggs lightly. Add enough water to make 3 cups.
Add remaining ingredients. Pour into individual cups and
steam until egg is firm.

For variety, substitute bamboo shoots for peanuts.
Serves 6.

STEAMED EGG CUP II

JAPAN

3 large eggs
3¼ cups meat stock
1 tsp. salt
2 tsp. soy sauce
5 tsp. sherry or other
    light wine
⅛ cup raw chopped
    spinach

¼ raw chicken, sliced
    very thin or white fish,
    sliced very thin or
    cleaned and deveined
    raw shrimp (combine,
    if desired)
6 small dried mushrooms,
    softened in warm water

Combine eggs, meat stock, salt, soy sauce and sherry
and divide into 6 custard cups.

Distribute meat or fish, mushrooms and chopped spinach
evenly among the 6 cups and cover each with aluminum
foil.

Steam on a rack over boiling water for about 20 minutes.
Serves 6.

EGG FOO YUNG

CHINA

1 cup cooked mush-
    rooms
2 tbs. butter
¼ cup minced onion
1 tbs. soy sauce
¼ tsp. salt

1½ cups bean sprouts,
    drained
6 eggs, beaten
1 cup shredded cooked
    lobster
¼ cup peeled diced
    water chestnuts

Slice mushrooms thin. Saute 5 minutes in butter. Combine with remaining ingredients and blend together. This recipe calls for Japanese or Chinese soy sauce. American brands are concentrated and very salty; therefore use only a few drops of them, tasting frequently to judge the amount.

Heat a small amount of oil in a shallow pan. Drop mixture by spoonfuls into the hot oil. Brown on one side, then turn to complete browning. Serve hot with the following sauce.

Sauce

In a cup combine 1½ tsp. cornstarch with 1 tbs. cold water. Stir into 1 cup of boiling meat stock. Cook 5 minutes, stirring constantly. Add ¼ tsp. sugar, ¼ tsp. salt and 1 tbs. soy sauce.

TEA EGGS

CHINA

12 medium eggs
2 tbs. black tea
2 tbs. anise cloves

2 tbs. soy sauce
4 tsp. salt

Hard boil the eggs about 25 minutes, starting in cold water. Cool eggs in cold water for 5 minutes.

Make cracks in the shells by rolling firmly on the table.

Place eggs and all ingredients in a pan and add sufficient water to cover. Cook and simmer for 1 hour. Serves 6.

CURRIED EGGS

AFRICA

Sister Margaret Hart, serving in Africa, tells us that this is a good dish to serve when eggs are available. Locally it is served with rice or ugali, a thick cornmeal mush made from freshly ground dried corn.

1 grated coconut	1 tsp. curry powder
2 cups boiling water	1 tsp. butter
3 large tomatoes, peeled	Salt to taste
2 medium onions	6 hard-boiled eggs

Grate the coconut and allow to soak in the boiling water. When cooled, drain and set aside the liquid. Discard the coconut pulp.

Chop together the onions and tomatoes.

In a large saucepan, bring the coconut water to a boil.

Add the chopped tomatoes and onions, butter and curry powder. Cook until the mixture has begun to thicken. Add salt to taste.

Peel the hard-boiled eggs and simmer in the mixture for 10 minutes. Serve with rice or ugali (page 150).

HUEVOS A LA RANCHERA

GUATEMALA

4 cups tomatoes, chopped fine	Round hot chili peppers, to taste
½ cup onions, chopped very fine	Salt and pepper to taste
	1 tbs. fat or salad oil
2 cloves garlic, minced	8 eggs

In a frypan, fry together all the above ingredients except the eggs in a tbs. of fat or oil until cooked. Set aside.

Break eggs into a hot, greased skillet as though to fry, then immediately pour sauce on top and cook until done to taste. Serves 6.

OYAKO DOMBURI

JAPAN

This recipe was sent by Sister Yae Ono, who has been working in Japan for many years. The name denotes "parent-child" bowl, with the chicken as the parent and the egg as the child.

1 lb. chicken, sliced in small thin pieces	½ bamboo shoot, sliced lengthwise
4 small onions, cut lengthwise	⅓ cup soy sauce mixed with ½ cup sugar
5 dried mushrooms	4 eggs

Fry the chicken in a little oil. When it begins to brown, add onions and other vegetables. Cook 2 minutes, then add seasonings. Cook another 20 minutes. Add ½ cup water to make stock.

Beat eggs lightly and pour over the above mixture. Cover the pan and continue cooking until the eggs are set. Cut into serving size pieces and serve over individual bowls of hot steamed rice. Serves 6.

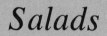

Salads

QUEEN EMMA'S AVOCADO SALAD

HAWAII

1 cup chopped crab or
  shrimp
2 green onions, chopped
  fine
1 tbs. prepared mustard
½ tsp. salt
3 avocados, dipped in
  lemon juice
2 peeled tomatoes,
  cubed

1½ cups celery, finely
  cubed
2 tbs. lemon juice
½ tsp. black pepper
Mayonnaise
Capers
Crisp lettuce and water-
  cress greens

Mix olive oil, mustard and vinegar. Add remaining seasonings and toss crab, tomato, onion and celery well into the mixture. To serve, arrange avocados on crisp lettuce leaf and pile crab mixture in the center of the avocado. Place small puff of mayonnaise on top and sprinkle with several capers. Garnish with watercress. Serves 6.

CEVICHE

PERU

This very old Peruvian recipe is prepared for almost every big fiesta, even today. It's also a delicious way to serve fish on a warm day. This pickled fish dish is one of Sister Carol Cannon's favorites.

2 lbs. sole or flounder or
  other white fish
1 cup fresh lime juice
1 cup fresh lemon juice
2 red or Spanish onions

½ tsp. chopped garlic
1 tsp. salt
Pepper to taste
Chili peppers, to taste

Peruvians like hot, spicy food and so use a very hot chili pepper (usually dried) for this dish. To make the dish less spicy, fewer peppers may be used or they may be soaked and boiled a few times, changing the water each time to decrease their potency. Peruvians use about 4 long chili peppers (yellow or red), removing the seeds, then pounding to a powder.

To prepare, mix the ground peppers with the lemon and lime juices, salt, garlic and black pepper.

Cut the fish into 1 inch cubes. Pour the liquid over the fish in a glass bowl and marinate for at least 2 hours. The dish should be covered and refrigerated.

When the fish is white and opaque, it is ready to use, similar to pickled herring. The onions are sliced and soaked in salted water for a few minutes, then mixed with the fish and served on lettuce. Or if preferred, the onions can be marinated with the fish. Serves 8.

SALAD DRESSING

CHINA

A tasty salad dressing that's also delicious served over leftover meats. If fresh ginger is not available, it can be omitted from the recipe.

1 tsp. ginger root	*3 tbs. soy sauce*
3 tbs. vinegar	*1 tbs. sugar*

Chop fresh ginger into small pieces and mix into any vegetable salad greens. Then mix in a bowl the vinegar, soy sauce and sugar. Spread over salad just before serving.

CINCAMA SALAD

PHILIPPINES

In some mission areas, familiar fruits and vegetables are not always available. Sister Edna Foster sent this improvisation for Waldorf Salad from the Philippines, where the local vegetable, cincamas, has been substituted for apples. (If you happen to run out of cincamas, of course, you can always use apples.)

Also, use cashew nuts in place of walnuts. Omit the celery (unless you live in Baguio or other places where it is available) and proceed with your favorite recipe for Waldorf Salad. Add 1 tablespoon of salamancie juice.

Quantities will depend on the number of people to be served (and how close you are to Manila).

SUNOMONO SALAD

JAPAN

¼ cucumber
1 fresh persimmon
1 tsp. grated horseradish
1 tsp. grated ginger root

⅛ cup sugar
Pinch of salt
¼ cup vinegar
8 medium radishes

Mix sugar and salt into vinegar. Pare radishes and grate finely, adding them to the vinegar. Cut cucumbers into ⅛ inch cubes. Dice the persimmon slightly larger. (Boiled shrimp may be substituted for persimmon.)

Combine cucumber, persimmon, freshly grated horseradish and freshly grated ginger root. Season to taste with soy sauce.

Shape into mounds on individual salad plates. Garnish with sesame seed, ground peanuts or walnuts, caviar, or soybean cake. Serves 4.

ONION SALAD

CEYLON

1 large onion, peeled
1 medium cucumber
1 medium green pepper
3 hard-boiled eggs,
   peeled

Juice of ½ lemon
½ tsp. salt
½ tsp. black pepper

Finely slice the onion, cucumber and green pepper. Remove seeds from pepper. Mix in bowl. Add lemon juice, salt and black pepper. Toss lightly.

Cut eggs in half and arrange on onion mixture. Chill in refrigerator until ready to serve. Used particularly as an accompaniment to curry and rice dishes. Serves 6.

ANDEAN SALAD

CHILE

2 cups cooked or canned
  chick peas
½ lb. cream cheese
2 medium onions, thinly
  sliced

½ cup olive oil
½ cup lemon juice
1 tsp. salt.
½ tsp. ground coriander
6 hard-boiled eggs

In a bowl, combine the chick peas, cheese and onions.

In a second bowl, combine the rest of the ingredients, except the eggs, and mix well. Pour this mixture over the chick pea mixture.

Chill and serve in lettuce cups garnished with hard-boiled egg wedges. Serves 6.

BACHELOR'S SALAD

BOLIVIA

The Bolivians call this "Bachelor's Salad" because it is easy to make and needs no cooking.

2 cups cottage cheese,
  drained
Salt and pepper to taste
1 chopped medium onion

1 cup chopped tomatoes
1 tbs. chopped pimento
  or parsley

Chill drained cottage cheese in refrigerator. Cream the cheese with a fork until smooth. Season to taste. Mix in onions and tomatoes. Mold in custard cups and rechill.

Serve over lettuce leaves garnished with a finely chopped hot pepper called locato (although parsley or pimento may be substituted). Serves 4.

KACHAMBALI

TANZANIA

Sister Ruth Naegle taught in Tanzania for several years and also directed the girls who prepared the meals for the students in the Maryknoll school there. She tells us this favorite salad is served frequently.

2 cups tomato wedges
½ tsp. salt

2 cups onions, sliced from
    top to bottom

Combine tomato wedges and sliced onion. Stir gently to mix well and sprinkle with salt. Allow to stand for a while to allow flavors and juices to mingle. Serves 6.

AVOCADO SALAD

GUATEMALA

2 avocados
2 hard-boiled eggs
3 small tomatoes
6 stuffed olives
Sliced bacon

1 small onion
French dressing
Fresh chili pepper or
    chili powder

Dice avocados, eggs and tomatoes. Slice olives and mince the onion. Combine and mix well. Add French dressing to moisten. Season to taste with chili. Serve on lettuce with bacon. Serves 6.

SHRIMP SALAD

BURMA

1½ lbs. uncooked shrimp,
    shelled and deveined
Boiling water
Salt
Juice of 1 lime

½ cup finely chopped
    onion
Salt and pepper to taste
Lettuce leaves

Cover shrimp with boiling water that has been salted (1 tsp. salt per quart water). Lower heat, cover and simmer for 7 minutes. Drain and chop shrimp.

Combine the finely chopped shrimp, onion, lime juice, salt and pepper. Toss lightly and chill. Serve on crisp lettuce leaves. Serves 4–6.

MU SAINGCHAI

KOREA

A turnip salad with a tangy taste. Excellent for a warm day.

5 medium turnips, sliced	1½ tbs. sugar
2 cups sliced apple or pear	1 tsp. salt
	2½ tbs. vinegar
1⅓ tbs. chopped green onions with tops	1½ tsp. sesame or salad oil
3 tbs. white sesame seeds, browned and pulverized	1 or 2 small red peppers, to taste
	1 tbs. soy sauce

Cut turnips into very thin strips and sprinkle with salt. After 15 minutes, squeeze out excess liquid.

Place turnips into a bowl. Add vinegar, onion, oil, soy sauce and seasame seeds. Mix well. Pare apple, cut into strips and add to mixture. Garnish with shredded red pepper and serve cold. Serves 6.

ESCABECHE DE GALLINA

PERU

This recipe for pickled chicken salad is well known throughout South America. Peruvians serve it on any festive occasion.

1 chicken cut in pieces	2 large onions
1 cup dry white wine	2 carrots
1 cup white vinegar	¼ tsp. thyme

2 leeks cut in 1-inch
  lengths
3 tsp. salt
2 stalks celery cut in
  1-inch lengths

2 bay leaves
Parsley sprigs
1 lemon, cut in slices

Fry the chicken in an oiled skillet until browned. Add wine, vinegar and water mixed with the seasonings. Cut the onions in wedges, the carrots into ½ inch slices, and place them and the rest of the ingredients (except the lemon) over the chicken. Cover and steam until the chicken and vegetables are tender.

Place the chicken and vegetables in a deep serving bowl. Strain the liquid over it. Cool, then refrigerate until the broth has jelled. Garnish with lemon slices and parsley sprigs. Serves 6.

PAPAS A LA HUANCAINA

PERU

This potato salad is a favorite Peruvian dish served on all fiesta occasions. It was submitted by Sister Ruth Marie Wohlfrom who has served for many years in South America, first in Bolivia and now in Peru.

10 medium potatoes
Sauce
2 cups fresh cheese
3 hard-boiled egg yolks
2 tbs. ground hot pepper
Salt and pepper to taste
1 cup salad oil
10 large ripe olives

½ cup condensed milk
A few drops lemon juice
¼ cup onion, finely
  chopped and rinsed
  in boiling water
5 sliced hard-boiled eggs
1 hot pepper or pimento,
  into strips

Cook potatoes in boiling water to which a bit of salt has been added. Cool and peel potatoes.

To make the sauce, mash together the cheese and the hard-boiled egg yolks, using a fork. Add ground hot pepper, salt, black pepper and mix well. Pour in oil, a little at a time as for mayonnaise, stirring constantly. Add the condensed milk, then the lemon juice slowly. Beat well. Lastly, add the onions.

To serve, arrange lettuce leaves on a platter and arrange peeled potatoes on them. Cover the potatoes with the sauce and garnish with the sliced hard-boiled eggs, sliced peppers and olives. Serve cold. Serves 8.

O I NAMUL

KOREA

3 cups sliced cucumber
1 tbs. coarsely crushed
    salt
1 cup water
2 tbs. vinegar
1 tbs. soy sauce
½ tsp. sugar
2 tsp. white sesame seed,
    browned and
    pulverized

¼ tsp. red or cayenne
    pepper
¼ tsp. finely chopped
    garlic
2 tbs. finely chopped
    green onions with tops

Remove rind from cucumbers and cut into slices. Sprinkle with salt and add 1 cup water. Soak cucumbers for 15 minutes and drain off as much liquid as possible.

Add other ingredients, mix thoroughly, chill and serve. Serves 6.

VIETNAMESE SALAD DRESSING

1 lb. tender beef, cubed
2 cloves garlic, crushed
½ cup soy sauce
¼ tsp. sugar

Dash black pepper
Dash salty sauce
Vinegar as needed

Combine garlic, soy sauce, sugar, salt and pepper. Marinate beef 15 minutes before cooking.

Heat 3–4 tbs. oil in a heavy skillet. Add beef and cook 5 minutes over high heat. Cool. Add vinegar. Serve over greens as a salad dressing.

VERDURA CON MAYONESA Y POLLO

GUATEMALA

Ana Ingrid Lange brought this chicken and vegetable salad to a picnic in Guatemala. It made such a hit that Sister Benigna Foley asked her for the recipe. The recipe can be increased according to the number of people served and allows for a great deal of variation.

¼ cup ejote (Mexican string beans)
¼ cup carrots
¼ cup cabbage
¼ cup peas
2 tbs. vinegar
Salt and pepper to taste
1 lb. cooked chicken, cut in bite-size pieces

1 cup mayonnaise
1 tbs. powdered mustard
½ cup celery, diced
¼ cup pimentos, sliced fine
1 tbs. finely chopped parsley

Slice finely the carrots, string beans and cabbage, add the peas and cook in a small amount of water. When vegetables are cooked, drain and set aside to cool. Add vinegar, salt and pepper. Mix well and chill in refrigerator.

Just before serving, mix vegetables with chicken and mask with mayonnaise to which has been added 1 tbs. powdered mustard.

Add celery, pimento and parsley, mix well and serve. Serves 4–6.

LUAU STYLE PINEAPPLE

HAWAII

Kaneohe, where Sister Joan Uhlen was stationed, is famous for its annual parish luau, attended by hundreds of Marines and Marine families, tourists and luau-lovers from all over the island of Oahu. The Sisters and students with their families prepare the feast. The following is always a favorite among the guests.

To prepare a pineapple luau-style, cut a thick slice from top and bottom. Cut out center in one solid cylinder. Cut cylinder in 2, lengthwise, and remove the core. Slice cylinder halves into lengthwise spears and refill the shell of the pineapple. Replace top and serve with fork. One pineapple serves 8–10.

To prepare pineapple family-style, cut a thick slice from top and bottom. Peel entire pineapple thickly from the top down. Remove "eyes" by cutting grooves diagonally. Slice in ½ inch slices, or lengthwise spears. Remove core. Add sugar, if necessary. Chill and serve. One pineapple serves 6–8.

PEANUT BUTTER SALAD

INDONESIA

½ lb. cabbage	1 tsp. lemon juice
½ lb. string beans	1 tsp. soy sauce
1 lb. bean sprouts	1 sliced onion, fried
1 cucumber, sliced	2 small hot peppers
1 tsp. salt	¼-½ lb. peanut butter
2 tsp. brown sugar	2 hard-boiled eggs

Cut cabbage and string beans and parboil with the bean sprouts. Save the cooking water.

Slice the cucumber and radishes.

In a bowl prepare the peanut butter sauce by mixing and crushing in order the salt, sugar, lemon juice, soy sauce, onions, hot peppers and peanut butter. Add ½ cup of the warm vegetable water.

Garnish with sliced hard-boiled eggs. Serves 6.

TROPICAL FRUIT SALAD

HAWAII

Cut up bite-sized pieces of fresh fruit for 6 salads using melon, bananas, pineapple, watermelon, mangoes, seedless grapes, nectarines, papaya and tangerines. Peel melon and cut in slices. Peel bananas and halve lengthwise. Sprinkle with lemon juice to minimize discoloration. Peel and cube pineapple. Halve grapes.

Use alternate slices of fruit, arranged nicely and serve with shredded coconut sprinkled on top. Chill before serving.

As a dressing, mayonnaise seasoned with curry powder may be served separately. Or combine ½ cup of any fruit juice, 3 tbs. each of lemon juice and sugar, and ¾ cup olive oil. Mix ingredients with 1 cup sour cream.

Salad may be served on a bed of greens in individual salad plates or from the bowl. Serves 6.

POMELO AND BANANAS

PHILIPPINES

1 pomelo, peeled   1 tbs. sugar
2 sliced bananas

Peel pomelo with care. Remove segments with the fingers from its white membrane. Place segmented pomelo in a fruit bowl. Add sugar and mix carefully. Then add sliced bananas, again mixing carefully but thoroughly so that bananas will not turn brown.

Refrigerate and serve cold. It makes a good luncheon salad or breakfast food. Serves 6.

SPINACH SALAD

CHINA

1 lb. fresh spinach   ½ cup white sesame
1 quart boiling water   seeds, browned and
2 tbs. soy sauce   pulverized
1 tbs. sugar   2 tbs. vinegar
Salt and pepper to taste   Ginger to taste

Mix soy sauce, sugar, sesame paste, vinegar, ginger, salt and pepper into a dressing.

Wash spinach thoroughly, using only the leaves. Pour boiling water over the leaves to cause them to wilt. Drain and chill in the refrigerator.

Serve with above dressing. Serves 6.

Note: ½ cup peanut butter may be substituted for the pulverized sesame paste.

K'ONG NAMUL I

KOREA

A cold delicious bean sprout salad. A hot version of this traditional dish, K'ong Namul II, appears on page 149.

1 lb. fresh or 4 cups canned bean sprouts	1 tbs. white sesame seed, browned and pulverized
1 tsp. salt	
2 cups boiling water	3 tbs. soy sauce
1½ tbs. chopped green onions with tops	⅛ tsp. garlic, chopped fine
½ tsp. sugar	Pinch of cayenne pepper
1 tbs. sesame oil	

Clean fresh bean sprouts and wash in cold water. Cook in salted boiling water for 2 minutes. If canned bean sprouts are used, omit the cooking step.

Add seasoning, mix well and serve cold. Serves 6.

EGGPLANT SALAD

ARMENIA

1 medium eggplant, about 1½ lbs.	4 minced garlic cloves
	2 tsp. paprika
2 sliced medium onions	1 cup olive oil
2 chopped tomatoes	1½ cups water
½ cup chopped parsley	1 tsp. salt
Dash of black pepper	

Remove stem from eggplant, wash and quarter. On either

side of each wedge or quarter make a deep slash.

Mix all ingredients except oil and water and stuff slashes or pockets with the mixture.

Place eggplant in baking pan to which the oil and water have been added. Cover pan with aluminum foil and bake in a moderate oven for 2½ hours, basting occasionally. Cool and chill before serving. Serves 4.

Meat Dishes

PORK AND VEGETABLE PIE

CHINA

1 lb. pork spareribs,
 cubed
1 tbs. soy sauce
1 tbs. fish sauce, patis
 (optional)
2 tbs. cornstarch
 solution
¼ cup slivered carrots
½ cup dried Chinese
 mushrooms, soaked
 and halved
2 stalks celery, sliced
¼ tsp. white pepper
1 tbs. brown sugar

1 tbs. soy sauce
1 cup meat broth
¼ cup spring onions,
 chopped
3 tbs. water
1 tsp. brown sugar
¾ cup shortening
1¼ cups flour
1 duck's egg yolk or 1
 large chicken's egg
 yolk

Marinate the pork in soy sauce, fish sauce and the cornstarch solution.

Blanch the carrots, Chinese mushrooms and celery. Drain in a colander.

Deep fat fry the pork cubes in hot oil, stirring constantly. Remove from oil and allow to drain on vegetables in colander.

Place pork and vegetables in a heavy skillet. Saute and season with white pepper, sugar, soy sauce, fish sauce and cornstarch solution.

Add broth to the skillet. Transfer mixture to a shallow baking dish, garnish with onions and set aside.

To make dough for the crust mix water and 1 tsp. sugar in a bowl and stir until sugar is dissolved. Add the shortening and flour. Knead with the fingers until smooth.

Sprinkle flour on pastry board and roll dough into a round piece slightly larger than the baking dish. Fold in half and cut 5 slits in the middle of the dough.

Cover the pie filling and crimp the edges with fingers. Brush surface with egg yolks. Bake in 350°F oven for 15 minutes. Serves 8–12.

FRIED LUMPIA

PHILIPPINES

1 lb. ground pork
1 lb. chopped shrimp
½ cup chopped
   mushrooms
3 egg yolks
Pepper and salt to taste

2 eggs, separated
½ cup cornstarch
2 cups water
1 cup vinegar
1 cup tomato catsup

To make filling, steam together the pork, shrimp, mushrooms, egg yolks, salt and pepper until the meat is cooked. Form into very small rolls and wrap in lumpia wrappers.

To make wrappers, beat the 2 egg whites until frothy. Add the 2 egg yolks and blend them together. Mix cornstarch with 1 cup water and add to egg mixture. Cook as you would a pancake in a greased, hot skillet. Spoon 2 tbs. of the batter mixture in the hot pan and tilt pan to spread batter evenly. Cook until slightly brown. Remove from pan and roll meat mixture inside. Repeat until all meat mixture has been used. Fry rolls in deep fat and serve with sweet-sour sauce below.

To prepare sweet-sour sauce, mix vinegar, catsup and 1 cup water. Add sugar, salt, pepper and chopped garlic to taste. Heat slowly until it reaches a boil. Thicken with a small amount of cornstarch. Serves 4–6.

LIMA TRIPE

PERU

1 lb. fresh tripe
2 tbs. olive oil
1 small onion, minced
1 tbs. ground hot yellow
   pepper

1 clove garlic, minced
¼ tsp. palillo
1½ tbs. parsley, minced
Salt and pepper to taste
1 lb. potatoes, cubed

Cook tripe in salted water until tender. Remove and cut into bite-sized pieces.

Heat oil in a large skillet and fry tripe along with the onions, yellow pepper, garlic, palillo, parsley, salt and pepper. Add potatoes and mix well. Add a little of the water in which the tripe was cooked and simmer until the potatoes are cooked and the liquid is absorbed. Serve hot with rice and garnish with lemon slices. Serves 4.

SWEET-SOUR PORK

CHINA

1½ lbs. pork shoulder, cut in 1-inch pieces
½ cup mushrooms
Water
1 green pepper, cut in strips
1 sliced medium onion

¼ cup unsulfured molasses
2 tsp. soy sauce
¼ cup vinegar
1 tbs. cornstarch
3 cups hot cooked rice

Brown meat in skillet. Drain mushrooms and measure liquid. Add enough water to make 1 cup. Add to skillet and bring to a boil. Cover, reduce heat and simmer for 45 minutes.

Add mushrooms, pepper and onion. Mix together molasses, soy sauce and vinegar. Add to skillet and cook 15 minutes longer, stirring occasionally. Blend cornstarch with a small amount of cold water. Stir into hot mixture. Cook, stirring until slightly thickened.

Serve with hot cooked rice. Serves 4.

PORK TOCHINO

PHILIPPINES

Sister Patricia Noble, intrigued by this feast day dish, obtained the recipe from Miss Clotilde Corpen who has been cooking for the Maryknoll Sisters in Manila for over 30 years.

1 lb. thinly sliced lean pork

¼ cup soy sauce
1 clove garlic, minced

½ cup catsup   Salt and pepper to taste

Combine the soy sauce, garlic, catsup, salt and pepper. Pour over sliced pork in a bowl, cover, refrigerate and marinate the pork in the sauce overnight.

Fry or broil the pieces of pork, basting occasionally with the marinade.

When cooked, place on a large platter, garnish with french-fried onions and quartered tomatoes. Serves 6.

SWEET AND PUNGENT PORK

CHINA

Mrs. Thomas Yang, a former student of Sister Mary Corde Lorang, sent this recipe from Stockton, California, where she now lives with her family.

1 egg	3 large green peppers,
2 tbs. flour	cut in sixths
½ tsp. salt	4 slices pineapple
Dash black pepper	1 cup chicken bouillon
¾ cup cooking oil	2½ tbs. cornstarch
1 tsp. salt	2 tsp. soy sauce
1 clove garlic, diced	½ cup vinegar
1 lb. lean pork	½ cup sugar

Prepare a batter from the egg, flour, ½ tsp. salt and a dash of pepper.

Heat oil in a heavy skillet. Add salt and the diced garlic.

Dip pork in the batter to cover well. Brown each piece in the hot oil. Pour off all the oil except for 1 tbs.

Cook pepper in boiling water about 8 minutes or until tender. Drain.

Add to browned pork the cooked peppers, pineapple and ⅓ cup chicken stock. Cook 10 minutes.

In a separate bowl, thoroughly blend cornstarch, soy sauce, vinegar, sugar and remainder of chicken broth. Add to the ingredients in the skillet, stirring constantly, until the juice thickens and the mixture is very hot. Serves 4.

SWEET AND SOUR PORK I

CHINA

2 lbs. lean pork
2 cups oatmeal
1 cup flour
3 tbs. cornstarch
1 tsp. salt
Pepper to taste
2 eggs, beaten
Water

Sauce
4 cups pineapple juice

1 cup dill pickle juice
1 tsp. vinegar
Sugar to taste
Catsup and hot sauce
 to taste
2 tsp. cornstarch
1 cup hot water
3 sliced tomatoes
1 cup diced pineapple
1 cup shredded green
 peppers

Cut the pork into serving sized pieces.

Prepare batter from oatmeal, flour, cornstarch, salt, pepper, eggs and enough water to make a liquid mixture.

Dip pork into batter and deep fat fry until thoroughly cooked and crisp.

To prepare the sweet-sour sauce, heat pineapple juice, pickle juice, vinegar, sugar, catsup, hot sauce, cornstarch and water in the upper part of a double boiler. Heat ingredients until mixture reaches a boil. Add tomatoes, diced pineapple and green peppers. Cook 5 minutes longer and serve hot over the fried pork. Serves 6.

SWEET AND SOUR PORK II

Broth from meat.

2½ lbs. slice from pork
 shoulder, boned
2 cups water
1 tsp. salt
4 tbs. soy sauce
2 tbs. sherry

Sauce

⅓ cup sugar

4 tbs. cornstarch

4 tbs. cider vinegar

⅓ cup pineapple juice
 (drained from 9 oz.
 can pineapple tidbits)

⅔ cup pineapple tid-
 bits (remainder of
 above can)

Cut meat into 1-inch cubes. Put into 2-quart saucepan. Add water, salt and soy sauce. Bring to a rolling boil over high heat. Cover and simmer for about 50 minutes (or until tender). Drain off meat broth into a small pan, skim off any floating fat and add sherry to broth.

In another saucepan, blend sugar, cornstarch, vinegar and pineapple juice, until smooth. Slowly stir into broth. Stir over medium-high heat until sauce is thick and translucent (about 5 minutes). Pour over pork cubes. Add pineapple tidbits and mix well. Serve warm. Serves 8.

PORK BALINESE

BALI

1 lb. pork	¼ lb. bamboo shoots,
2 tsp. salad oil	sliced 1-inch long
¼ lb. celery, chopped	1 lb. bean sprouts,
¼ lb. onions, chopped	drained
¼ lb. water chestnuts,	1 cup chicken broth
sliced	1 tsp. salt
¼ lb. mushrooms, sliced	2 tsp. cornstarch

Cut pork into 1 inch squares and saute in oil (or butter). Add vegetables, salt and chicken broth. Cook about 5 minutes over medium heat. Mix cornstarch with water and blend into sauce to thicken. Serves 4.

BROILED PORK

CHINA

1 lb. lean pork	2 tbs. salt
6 tbs. soy sauce	1 tsp. black pepper
2 tbs. sugar	

Cut meat into strips about 2 inches thick. Soak meat in mixture made with soy sauce, sugar, salt and pepper.

String the strips of meat on a wire or skewer and broil over a glowing charcoal fire. If a charcoal fire is not convenient, place strips of meat in a pan and broil under a gas flame until meat is well done and golden brown. Serve hot. Serves 4–6.

SWEET-SOUR SAUCE

CHINA

This delicious recipe for a basic sweet-sour sauce was sent to us by Sister Margaret Marie Jung and can be used to prepare tasty dishes with pork, beef or fish.

3 tbs. brown sugar
2 tsp. cornstarch
½ tsp. salt
1-1½ cups water
2 large tomatoes
2 slices canned pine-
*   apple*

3 tbs. sugar
½-¾ cups vinegar
½ small onion, sliced
*   and browned*
½ green pepper, sliced

In a medium size saucepan, mix all the dry ingredients. Stir in vinegar, slowly. Add water, stirring constantly to avoid lumping. Add the green pepper. Bring mixture to a boil over medium heat and add onion, tomatoes and pineapple. Cook for 10 minutes, then thicken with cornstarch.

For sweet-sour pork–Cut meat into 2-inch squares, salt and deep fat fry until cooked. Drain and cook in above sauce for 10 minutes. Serve hot with boiled rice. Serves 4 to 6.

For sweet-sour beef–Cut lean beef into small, thin slices. Season with salt and pepper. Add 1 tsp. soy sauce and fry in melted butter. When beef is browned, pour sweet-sour sauce into pan, stir and serve hot with boiled rice. Serves 4 to 6.

For sweet-sour fish–Use codfish. Remove bones and lay fish whole into a covered pan. Season with salt and 2 slices of fresh ginger root. Cover and steam cook until fish is white.

Remove ginger, pour sweet-sour sauce over fish and serve with boiled rice. Serves 4 to 6.

POLYNESIAN STEAK

HAWAII

Marinate a thick steak, large enough to serve 6, in marinade mixture for 2 hours. Combine the following ingredients in a bowl and mix:

Marinade
1 cup soy sauce	1 clove garlic
1 cup olive oil	⅛ tsp. ginger

Prepare the following sauce while the steak is marinating:

Sauce
2 onions, chopped	⅛ tsp. cinnamon
1 tbs. olive oil	1½ tsp. cornstarch
1 cup tomato sauce	1 cup beef gravy
½ cup marinade	1 cup crushed pineapple
1 tbs. curry powder	

Heat oil in a saucepan and cook onions until limp. Mix together all sauce ingredients except the cornstarch and pineapple. Bring mixture to a boil. Have ready a paste of cornstarch and 1 tbs. water. Add this to sauce, stirring constantly, and cook until thick. Salt to taste. Add canned pineapple and syrup.

Remove steak from marinade and broil. Serve with hot sauce. Serves 6.

SAMOSAS

AFRICA

Sister Patricia Hafey sent us the recipe for meat-filled turnovers, made by filling triangles of dough, then frying them. They are very hot as this is an Indian recipe, so go easy on the garlic and chili peppers.

Pastry
2 cups flour
Small amount of water
⅓ cup oil

Mix the flour and enough water to make a stiff dough. Tear dough into 8 equal-sized balls and roll out into 5 inch rounds. Brush each with a thin coating of oil and sprinkle with flour. Pile 4 rounds, one atop the other; then 4 more. Roll out each pile once more into 9 inch rounds. Cut the circle into 4 pie-shaped wedges. Peel off the layers, one by one, and fill with the following filling:

Filling
½ lb. ground meat
2 cloves garlic, crushed
2 tsp. chopped mint leaves
2 cups chopped onion
½ tsp. chopped chili pepper
½ tsp. cardamom
⅛ tsp. cloves
½ tsp. cinnamon

In a skillet, fry the meat in a little oil. Add the rest of the ingredients and cook until the meat is tender. Set aside to cool.

Fill pastry wedges with about 1 tablespoon of the meat mixture, seal the folds with a little water, and fry the Samosas in about 1½ inches of hot oil until brown on both sides. Drain and serve hot. Makes 24 turnovers.

SWEET AND SOUR SPARERIBS

CHINA

1½ lbs. spareribs
1 cup diced pineapple
½ cup mixed Chinese pickles
2 medium onions, sliced

2 green peppers, sliced
2 tsp. cornstarch
1½ tsp. sugar
1 tbs. lemon juice

1 tbs. soy sauce
Salt and pepper to taste
2 tbs. oil

Cook spareribs for 15 minutes in 1 quart boiling water. Drain and reserve liquid.

Heat oil in a skillet and fry together onions and green peppers until peppers are limp. Add 1½ cups sparerib broth, spareribs, pickles, sugar, soy sauce, salt and pepper. Add diced pineapple and lemon juice. Thicken gravy with cornstarch and serve hot with boiled rice. Serves 4.

MORCON

PHILIPPINES

A traditional Filipino recipe and a favorite of Sister Maria Concepcion Gallao. She tells us that grated Parmesan cheese may be substituted for the native Quese de Bola cheese.

2¼ lbs. lean round steak
¼ cup ground beef
¼ cup sweet pickles
2 tbs. seedless raisins
1 tsp. soy sauce
¼ cup ground ham
2 tbs. grated cheese
2 quartered hard-boiled eggs.
Juice of 3 limes

1 egg
2 cups water
¼ cup vinegar
1 sliced medium onion
2 cloves garlic
½ cup tomato sauce
1 small bay leaf
Salt, pepper and soy sauce

Slice meat into a sheet about ¼-inch thick, spread out and season with salt, pepper, lime juice and soy sauce.

Mix together ground beef, pickles, raisins, 1 tsp. soy sauce, ground ham, grated cheese, hard-boiled eggs, and raw egg. Season to taste and spread over meat. Roll as you would a jelly roll and secure with strong white thread.

Place in a deep pan and cover meat roll with water,

vinegar, onion, garlic, tomato sauce and bay leaf. Season with salt, pepper and soy sauce to taste. Simmer until tender.

To serve, drain, slice crosswise and serve with gravy. Serves 4.

TERIYAKI MEATS

JAPAN

Beef, fish, chicken or pork ribs fixed with teriyaki sauce are favorites in Japan. This recipe was sent to us by Sister Joan Uhlen.

1 lb. meat, cut into bite-sized pieces	1 tsp. grated fresh ginger (or less of powdered ginger)
½ cup soy sauce	
3 tbs. sugar	1 tbs. bourbon or wine
1 clove garlic, grated	

Marinate meat chunks at least 1 hour in teriyaki sauce made by combining all the other ingredients.

To serve, broil over charcoal or in a kitchen broiler. Serves 4.

SALTENAS

BOLIVIA

These meat turnovers are a popular "meal-in-one" in a number of South American countries. They are sold on street corners and in market stalls. Being quite hot, they usually are served with chilled beer. The filling actually allows for a great deal of variation from place to place.

Filling

½ cup chopped onions	2 tbs. raisins
1 tbs. salad oil	½ cup corn kernels
½ cup water	2 hard-boiled eggs, chopped
½ cup meat cut in tiny cubes	½ tsp. ground cummin

1 tsp. pulverized hot pepper	Black pepper to taste
	15 whole black olives

Saute onions and meat in the oil until slightly browned. Add the water, corn, seasonings and the raisins that have been puffed by soaking in hot water for a few minutes, then drained. Cook for 5 minutes, then remove from the heat. Cool slightly, then add the chopped hard-boiled eggs. Set aside while preparing the dough.

Dough

2 cups flour	½ cup plus 2 tbs. butter
1 tsp. salt	⅓ cup water

Mix as for pie crust. Roll to ⅛-inch thickness, then cut into rounds about 3-4 inches in diameter. Place about 1½ tbs. of the filling and 1 black olive in the center of each round. Fold over, seal opening by twisting slightly several times along the edge.

Arrange on a greased pan, placing the seal on top and flattening the opposite side. It looks like a tiny loaf with the twisted ridge down the middle of the top.

Bake for 10 minutes at 375°F until the pastry has cooked and the saltenas are browned. Serve hot. Makes about 15 turnovers.

TAMALES IN JACKETS

GUATEMALA

Drain canned tamales (the long, slender ones that come packed 5 or 6 to a 1 lb. can or jar), reserving sauce.

Remove paper wrappings. Wrap each tamale spirally in a strip of bacon.

Place tamales on a rack in a shallow pan. Bake at 425°F for 30 minutes.

In a saucepan, heat sauce in which tamales were packed. To serve, place tamales on platter or individual plates, cover with sauce and sprinkle with grated Parmesan cheese. Serve hot with chili beans and a green salad. Allow 2 tamales per person.

SHIN SU LO II

KOREA

Sister Augusta Hock spent many years in Korea and was often entertained as a dignitary by Korean officials. Now that she is back in the United States, her niece, Mrs. Larry Hock, prepares this variation of Shin Su Lo whenever she has the chance so that Sister will not be too lonesome for Korea.

1 boneless sirloin steak, (about 1½ lbs. cut 1-inch thick)	1 small yellow or zucchini squash
2 whole chicken breasts	¼ lb. fresh mushrooms
1 small eggplant	3½ cups chicken or beef broth
	½ lb. fresh spinach

Slice steak diagonally ¼-inch thick, then cut into bite-sized pieces.

Remove skin from chicken breasts. Remove bones and then slice into pieces ¼-inch thick. Cut into bite-sized pieces.

Arrange meats on plates and cover loosely. Chill until ready to serve.

Wash vegetables. Pare eggplant, quarter and slice into thin crescents. Trim ends of squash and cut into 2-inch long sticks. Trim stems from spinach and eliminate tough leaves. Place each vegetable in a separate plastic bag or bowl. Chill until ready to serve. To preserve their color, do not slice mushrooms until just before cooking.

Prepare dips as follows:

Peanut dip

Blend ¼ cup peanut butter with ½ cup hot water in a small saucepan. Stir in 1 tbs. molasses, 1 tbs. soy sauce, 1 clove minced garlic, a few drops of hot pepper seasoning and ½ tsp. lemon juice. Heat slowly, stirring constantly, to boiling. Simmer for 10 minutes or until slightly thick. Serve warm or chilled. Serves 6.

Soy dip

Combine ½ cup soy sauce, ¼ cup wine or cider vinegar and 1½ tsp. garlic powder in a small bowl. Chill until serving. Serves 6.

Hot-Hot sauce

Combine ⅓ cup chili sauce, 2 tbs. prepared horseradish, 1 tbs. lemon juice and ½ tsp. Worchestershire sauce in a small bowl. Chill until serving. Serves 6.

Chinese mustard dip

Stir ¼ cup boiling water into ¼ cup of dry English mustard until smooth. Stir in ½ tsp. salt and 2 tsp. salad oil. Serves 6.

About ½ hour before serving, arrange steak, chicken and vegetables in separate rows on a flat tray. Cover tray slightly and keep chilled.

Pour chicken or beef broth in your choice of table-top cooker. The ideal cooker is a Korean Shin Su Lo cooker with place in the center for charcoal. However, an electric skillet or chafing dish will do. Heat to simmering.

To serve, set cooker on the dining table beside the tray containing the meats and vegetables. Place small bowls of dips at convenient places on the table. Provide chopsticks or long handled forks for each guest.

Each guest picks up the meat or vegetable of his choice and cooks it in the simmering broth. Then he dips it into one of the dips and eats while hot. The meat strips cook in 1 to 2 minutes, the vegetables vary. Serves 6.

SOBORO GOHAN

JAPAN

1 lb. ground beef	*Boiled peas*
2 tsp. chopped ginger	*Boiled rice*
¼ cup sugar	*Shredded pickled red*
⅓ cup soy sauce	*ginger or pickled beets*
2 tbs. sake or sherry	

Fry ground beef in a heavy hot skillet for about 5 minutes. Add chopped ginger, sugar, soy sauce and sake.

Cook 5 minutes longer.

Place hot rice into 6 individual donburi bowls, about ⅔ full. Spoon meat mixture onto rice, garnish with red ginger or beets, cover and serve immediately. Serves 6.

CURRIED MEAT

TANZANIA

The amount of meat in this dish may vary depending on whether it is used for a sauce (somewhat as a spaghetti sauce) or as a main meat dish.

½ lb. meat cubed
1½ cups cubed
 tomatoes
1 cup cubed potatoes
½ cup onion

¾ cup tender okra pods
1 clove garlic, minced
1 tsp. curry powder
Salt to taste
2 tbs. butter

Cook the meat until tender. Remove from skillet.

Add butter to skillet and saute onions until soft. Add tomatoes and okra. When slightly cooked, return meat to the skillet. Add the remaining ingredients and cook until done, thickening at the last with a little flour mixed with water. Serves 3-4.

CHICHIN KOKI

KOREA

1½ lbs. tenderloin or
 round steak
½ tsp. sugar
1 tbs. white sesame seed,
 browned and
 pulverized
¼ tsp. black pepper

2 medium onions,
 sliced thin
¼ cup soy sauce
1½ tbs. sesame or
 salad oil
⅛ tsp. garlic
½ tsp. chopped ginger
 root

Wipe meat with a damp cloth. Cut into 2 inch squares ¼ inch thick. Pound and score meat.

Combine sugar, soy sauce, garlic and sesame seed. Pour this mixture over the meat and mix thoroughly.

Heat oil in a heavy skillet and fry meat, turning from time to time until cooked. Remove meat from pan and fry onions in the same oil.

Place onions on top of meat and serve hot. Serves 6.

FRIED EMPANADAS

GUATEMALA

Pastry	Filling
1 cup flour	1 lb. ground meat
½ tsp. salt	Black pepper to taste
1 tsp. baking powder	3 tbs. tomato paste
2 tbs. shortening	Salt to taste
⅓ cup milk	1 tbs. shortening
	2 tbs. chopped onion
	1 tbs. chili powder

Heat shortening in a large skillet, and saute meat and onion until brown. Add tomatoes, chili powder and season with salt and pepper. Cook for 15 minutes. Set aside.

To make pastry, mix together flour, salt, baking powder, shortening and milk. Knead as for biscuits, but roll out dough paper thin. Cut into large round circles.

Place a spoonful of meat mixture on pastry, fold over and press edges together with a fork.

Fry rapidly in deep fat until brown. Serve hot. Serves 25.

PORK ADOBO

PHILIPPINES

2 lbs. lean pork	2 tbs. butter
½ cup vinegar	Salt and pepper to taste
2 tbs. soy sauce	

Cut pork into 2-inch cubes. Soak in vinegar, crushed garlic, salt and pepper. Transfer to a deep saucepan and simmer covered until beef is tender. Reserve liquid.

Transfer beef to a large skillet containing melted butter. Add soy sauce and brown pork. Add the liquid in which the pork was cooked. Continue cooking until liquid has been reduced to a thick brown sauce. Serve with fresh tomato salad. Serves 6.

ENBUTIDO

PHILIPPINES

2 lbs. ground pork
2 chorizos de Bilbao
  (Spanish sausages)
  chopped fine

1 cup bread crumbs,
  soaked in ½ cup milk
2 beaten eggs
3 tbs. seedless raisins
Salt and pepper to taste

Mix together all ingredients. Wrap in a clean piece of cheesecloth and tie securely at both ends.

Place in a pan with just enough chicken or meat broth to cover. Bring to a boil and simmer until done. Cool.

Just before serving, unwrap and slice into pieces. Serve with liver or tomato sauce.

To prepare sauce, boil broth in which meat roll was cooked, simmering it down to desired quantity. Thicken with chicken liver paste or tomato puree. Season to taste with salt and pepper. Serves 4.

CHIAO-TZU

CHINA

2 cups chopped Chinese
  cabbage
½ lb. ground beef
1 small onion, chopped
½ tsp. ginger, chopped

2 tsp. soy sauce

Pastry
1 cup flour
Water

Chop cabbage very finely and allow to stand for 20 minutes. Squeeze out excess liquid, reserving liquid for use in broth.

In a bowl mix chopped ginger, soy sauce, garlic, pork and beef.

To make dough, mix enough water with flour to make a stiff dough. Roll out paper thin and cut out 3 inch rounds with a cookie cutter.

To make dumplings, spoon about 1 tsp. of the meat mix into the center of each round and press dough into the shape of a half-moon.

Have a kettle boiling with about 6 inches of water. Drop in a few Chiao-tzu. When they come to the surface they should not be crowded one atop the other.

At the first boil, add enough cold water to sink the Chiao-tzu. The second time the boiling point is reached, they are cooked.

Repeat procedure until all dumplings are boiled.

Serve with vinegar and soy sauce. For variety the following fillings may be substituted: veal with cucumbers; string beans with chicken; or substitute celery for the Chinese cabbage. Serves 4.

KUN KOKI

KOREA

1½ lbs. tenderloin or round steak or 2 lbs. short ribs	1 tbs. sugar
	⅓ cup finely chopped onion
¼ cup soy sauce	4 tbs. finely chopped green onion with tops
3 tbs. sesame or salad oil	
3 tbs. white sesame seed, browned and pulverized	⅓ tsp. finely chopped garlic
	¼ tsp. black pepper

If short ribs are used, select ribs having a generous amount of meat. Trim and cut each rib apart.

If steak is used, clean, trim and cut into 3 inch by 4 inch by ⅓ inch thick pieces. Pound meat and score with a knife, slashing lengthwise and crosswise.

Combine all ingredients with meat and mix thoroughly. Allow to stand for 1 hour or more (or it may be broiled immediately).

Broil over charcoal, in a broiler, or panbroil in a skillet, turning until meat is cooked. Serves 6.

PIPIKAULA

HAWAII

A delicious recipe for a traditional Hawaiian specialty, jerked beef.

2 lbs. boneless sirloin sliced 1 to 1½-inches thick, with fat
1 cup soy sauce

1 tbs. rock salt
Juice of ½ lemon
Pepper to taste
1 tsp. sugar

Combine soy sauce, lemon, sugar, salt and pepper and mix into a sauce.

Cut beef into strips about 1½ inches wide. Pound slightly and put into a bowl large enough to hold the quantity stripped. Pour the sauce over the beef, rub into the strips of beef and let stand for about 1 hour.

Dry in hot sun about 2 days, making sure to keep beef out of the night air.

Broil, turning occasionally until beef is nicely browned. Delicious with baked sweet potatoes. Serves 8.

CHU PAO PA

CHINA

Filling

½ lb. minced chicken or beef, cooked
1 tbs. minced pork, cooked
1 tbs. chopped canned mushrooms

1 tbs. bamboo shoots
1 tbs. minced onion
1 tsp. soy sauce
2 cups chicken or beef stock

Dough

1½ cups flour
½ beaten egg
Warm water

Sift flour onto a board and add egg and enough water to make a stiff dough. Knead until smooth and allow to stand for 7 or 8 minutes before rolling. Roll out very thin and cut into rounds about 3½-inches across.

To prepare filling, mix all minced ingredients, soy sauce and a dash of pepper. Form into balls the size of a walnut. Place each ball into a round of dough, pinch edges together to seal and steam about 30 minutes over chicken or beef stock. Serve immediately with individual sauce cups into which Chu Pao Pa are dipped. Serves 4.

EGG AND MEAT ROLL

CHINA

4 eggs
2 tbs. water
¼ tbs. salt

Filling
*1 lb. ground lean pork
  with fat*
½ cup minced onion

Salt and pepper to taste
1 cup ground carrot
2 tbs. soy sauce
*2 cups Chinese cabbage,
  finely ground*
*½ cup puffed rice,
  pounded fine*

In a bowl, beat together eggs, water and salt. Cook into large pancakes in a greased heavy skillet. Do not turn pancake over. Make as many as required to serve guests.

To make filling, heat a little fat in a frypan. Add onions and meat and saute until brown. Add cabbage, carrots and seasonings. Cook 2 minutes, then set aside and allow to cool.

To make meat roll, place filling ¼ inch over pancake. Roll as a jelly roll. Using a sharp knife, cut each roll diagonally into thin slices. Place slices in a bowl and steam for ½ hour. Serves 8.

LENGUA MECHADA

PHILIPPINES

1 ox or beef tongue
6 strips bacon
½ cup white wine
5 tbs. butter
1 small can tomato
  sauce

Pinch of dry English
  mustard
1 small can mushrooms
1 clove garlic
Salt and pepper to taste

Scald the tongue and remove outer skin. Wash in cold water.

Make a pocket in the tongue and insert strips of bacon. Brown tongue in butter. Add chopped garlic and continue to fry until brown. Add mustard, salt and pepper to taste.

Transfer mixture to a kettle, add wine, cover and simmer until the tongue is tender. Add water as needed.

When cooked, remove from the kettle and slice into rounds. Melt butter in a skillet and saute tongue rounds with mushrooms for 5 minutes. Add tomato sauce and simmer 5 more minutes. Serve hot. Serves 4.

BROILED BEEF

KOREA

If you're looking for something different in a beef recipe, try this one for thin beef slices, Korean-style. Sister Sigrid Christine Ortis' years in Korea provided her with ample time to become an expert in Korean cooking.

1 lb. beef
4 tbs. sugar
2 tbs. sesame or
  salad oil
6 tbs. soy sauce
Pinch of pepper
1 green onion, chopped

1 clove garlic, chopped
4 tbs. white sesame
  seed, browned and
  pulverized
1 tbs. flour
Water

Cut beef into thin pieces 3-inches square. Add sugar and oil and mix well. Combine soy sauce, pepper, onions, garlic, sesame seed and flour and add to meat. Mix well and allow to stand for about 15 minutes.

Broil or fry in a small amount of oil until tender. If frying meat, add a small amount of water after meat is well browned, cover tightly and steam until meat is tender. Serve hot. Serves 6.

TAMALE PIE

GUATEMALA

1½ lbs. ground beef
5 tbs. salad oil
2 chopped onions
3 cloves garlic, minced
2 tbs. chili powder
2½ cups tomatoes, strained

2 tbs. salt
1½ cups pitted olives, cut coarsely
6 cups boiling water
2 cups yellow corn meal
½ cup grated cheese

Heat oil in a large skillet and brown beef. Add onion and garlic and cook until golden. Add salt, chili powder, tomatoes and olives. Cook very slowly for 1½ hours.

Slowly stir in corn meal. Cook 15 minutes longer, stirring constantly.

Line a greased baking dish with 1 inch layer of the mush. Pour in meat filling. Spread remaining cornmeal mixture on top. Bake for 1½ hours in a 325°F oven. During the last 15 minutes, sprinkle top of pie with grated cheese. Serves 6–8.

PULGOGI

KOREA

This barbeque dish is cooked in a special pan in Korea. The pan is made of brass with holes in the domed central area and is canted at the rim to catch the luscious drippings of the broiling meat.

An electric grill may be used, but these flavor-filled juices will be lost. Or you may use an electric table-top cooker. However, if you have a gourmet taste, purchase a Pulgogi pan and use charcoal.

1 lb. lean beef, sliced
   very thin and cut into
   2-inch squares
1 small onion, chopped
1 green onion, chopped
   with tops
½ pear, grated
¼ cup soy sauce

2 tbs. sugar
1 tbs. sesame or salad
   oil
½ tsp. pepper
1 tbs. sesame seed,
   browned and
   pulverized.

Combine all seasonings, stirring until sugar is dissolved. Marinate meat in mixture for an hour or until you are ready to cook it. Broil meat and serve as soon as it is done.

To serve, provide each person with a small dish of soy sauce in which he may dip the broiled meat when it is served. Guests may sweeten soy sauce to taste. Serves 3.

SANCHEK

KOREA

⅓ lb. lean beef
⅓ lb. lean pork
8 green onions with
   tops
3 tbs. soy sauce
½ tsp. finely chopped
   garlic
2 eggs
½ tsp. sugar
1 cup flour

¾ tsp. salt
4 tbs. sesame or salad
   oil
½ lb. celery cabbage, or
   white or green mustard
   cabbage
2 tbs. white sesame
   seed, browned and
   pulverized

Cut meat into strips ½-inch by 3-inches and ¼-inch thick. Cut cabbage into pieces of similar size and onions into 3-inch strips.

Combine meat and vegetables and season with garlic,

sesame seed, 2 tsp. oil, soy sauce and sugar. Push toothpicks through meat and cabbage arranged alternately.

Make a batter of eggs, flour and salt. Dip prepared meat and vegetables into batter and fry in remaining oil until thoroughly cooked. Remove toothpicks and serve hot. Serves 6.

ORIENTAL BEEF

JAPAN

For an Oriental taste thrill, try this on your own patio, broiled over white-hot charcoal. Hang a few Japanese lanterns and you'll think you're in Japan.

1½ lbs. tenderloin or round steak, sliced in ¾-inch slices
5 tsp. sugar
1 scallion, chopped

½ cup soy sauce
¼ cup sherry wine
1 clove garlic, chopped
½ tsp. cayenne pepper

Mix sugar, soy sauce, sherry, garlic, scallion and cayenne pepper. Put beef strips in a bowl and pour soy mixture over it for about ½ hour. Drain.

Heat a heavy skillet and saute meat with a little oil or butter. Heat sauce, pour over meat and serve with boiled rice or macaroni, a green salad and fresh fruit. Serves 6.

PAPAS RELLENAS

CHILE

2 lbs. potatoes, boiled and riced
½ cup flour
1 lb. ground beef
½ cup raisins, if desired

½ tsp. oregano
Salt and pepper to taste
Pinch of cummin
1 hard-boiled egg, chopped

Mix together the hot riced potatoes and flour. Knead until smooth. Set aside while preparing the filling.

To make filling, steam beef in a small amount of water for 15 minutes. Add oregano, salt, pepper, cummin, egg and raisins. Cook 5 minutes longer. Allow to cool.

Roll potato mixture out on a floured board to a thickness of about ¼ inch. Cut into 2½ inch squares.

Place one tablespoonful of the meat mixture in the center of each small square of dough, fold over, seal and roll well in flour. Fry in hot oil. Roll in powdered sugar, if desired.

A variation may be made by substituting the meat mixture with cheese, about a 1-inch cube per square of the potato mixture. Fry as above. Serves 6.

BAKED KIBBI

LEBANON

Wheat mixture	Filling
½ lb. finely crushed wheat	½ cup chopped onions
	2 tsp. shortening
1 lb. ground, lean lamb	¼ lb. ground, lean pork
4 tbs. grated onions	2 tbs. pine nuts
1 tsp. salt	¼ tsp. salt
¼ tsp. pepper	½ tsp. pepper
2 pinches cinnamon	1 tbs. shortening

To make the wheat mixture, soak the wheat in water to cover, for 30 minutes. While the wheat is soaking, make the filling.

Saute onions in shortening until light and brown. Add pork, pine nuts, salt and pepper. Cook and stir until meat is browned.

Now mix into the wheat, the lamb, grated onion, salt, pepper and seasoning of wheat mixture. Knead the mixture well.

Spread one-half of the wheat mixture in a small, well greased baking pan. Sprinkle with filling. Cover with the remaining meat mixture. Press whole down firmly.

With sharp knife, cut diagonal lines across the top to

make diamond shapes. Dot the top with a tablespoon of shortening. Bake in a pre-heated oven at 400° for 30 minutes. Then reduce the heat in the oven and bake 30 minutes longer. Serves 4.

Chicken and Other Fowl

YAKITORI

JAPAN

Yakitori, an authentic Japanese recipe contributed by Sister M. Tomi Nishimuto, means broiled chicken in that language. It is best prepared over a charcoal fire. However, a wood or gas flame can be used instead.

1 broiler (3-4 lbs.)	¼ cup sugar
10 large scallions	¾ cup sake or cooking
Cayenne pepper to taste	sherry
¾ cup soy sauce	

Cut chicken into 1½ inch squares. Then slice scallions into 2 inch lengths.

Skewer pieces of chicken and scallion alternately onto wooden or metal skewers about 6 inches long. Each skewer will usually take 4 pieces of chicken and 3 pieces of scallion. Chicken livers may also be used.

Mix soy sauce, sugar and saki and baste skewered food in sauce. Just before eating, broil over white glowing charcoal fire. Keep skewers about 4 inches above coals. Do not broil excessively. Serve hot sprinkled with cayenne pepper. Serves 4.

BURMESE CURRIED CHICKEN

1 stewing chicken (4 lbs.)	1 cup onion, chopped fine
Hot water	⅛ tsp. saffron
2 tbs. salt	1 tbs. cornstarch
¼ cup salad oil	¼ cup cold water
4 chili peppers	3 cups hot cooked rice

Place chicken in deep pot, cover with hot water, add salt and simmer until tender (about 2 hours). Drain chicken and save the broth.

Remove meat from bones and cube it. Heat salad oil in saucepan, adding finely crushed peppers, chopped onion and saffron. Cook until onion is soft. Add cubed chicken with 2 cups of the chicken broth and simmer for 20 minutes.

Meanwhile, blend ¼ cup of cold water with the cornstarch. Add to chicken mixture to thicken sauce. Continue cooking for 5 minutes, stirring constantly. Serve over hot rice. Serves 3 to 4.

CHINESE CHICKEN A LA KING

1 chicken (3-4 lbs.)	1 tsp. red bean powder
2 large green peppers	½ cup soy sauce
1 small onion	2 cups cooking sherry
2 tbs. bean flour	1 tsp. vinegar
3 tbs. lard	1 tsp. vegetable oil

Cut chicken into 1 inch squares. Roll chicken in the bean flour.

Heat lard in frypan. Fry chicken pieces until golden brown.

Chop green pepper and onions and add to frypan, stirring constantly until onion begins to brown.

Add oil, red bean powder, soy sauce, vinegar and sherry. Cover, simmer slowly until chicken is tender. Serves 4.

CHICKEN VELVET AND SNOW PEAS

CHINA

½ lb. chicken, white meat	½ tsp. cooking sherry
3 cups chicken broth	½ tsp. salt
3 egg whites	2 cups vegetable oil
2 tbs. cornstarch	½ lb. snow peas

Blend chicken meat in blender at low speed, adding 1 cup chicken broth gradually until chicken becomes a smooth paste. Pour into mixing bowl, discarding gristle if any. Fold in slightly beaten egg whites, 1 cup of chicken broth, cooking sherry, salt and 1 tbs. cornstarch.

Heat vegetable oil in a skillet. Spread the thin chicken mixture into the oil using a tablespoon. Immediately add another layer, and another. When the chicken mixture turns white, immediately remove skillet from the heat and place the cooked chicken into a strainer to drain off the oil. Repeat until all the chicken mixture has been cooked.

Fry the snow peas from 3 to 5 minutes in the oil drained from the cooked chicken. Add to the chicken.

Thicken 1 cup of chicken broth with 1 tbs. cornstarch and pour over chicken and snow peas. Serve hot. Serves 4.

CHICKEN CURRY

PAKISTAN

¼ lb. butter
½ cup chopped onion
1 chicken (3 lbs.)
1 cup yogurt
2 cups water
1 tsp. ground ginger
Salt and pepper to taste

1 tsp. turmeric powder
4 small green chili peppers, chopped
2 whole cardamoms and small stick cinnamon tied in cheesecloth

Melt butter in a large heavy kettle. Add onion and cook until tender.

Cut chicken into serving pieces. Remove onion and brown chicken in remaining butter. Return chicken to kettle and add yogurt, water, ginger and turmeric. Cook on medium heat for 15 minutes.

Add chili peppers and cheesecloth bag containing cardamom and cinnamon. Add salt and pepper. Cook another 15 minutes, or until chicken is tender. Remove cheesecloth bag before serving. Serve hot with boiled rice. Serves 6 to 8.

ARROZ CON PATO A LA PERUANA

PERU

This recipe for Peruvian duck with rice is a favorite of Sister Ruth Marie Wohlfrom.

1 duck, frozen
Salt and pepper to taste
½ cup vegetable oil
1 clove garlic, ground
1 chopped large onion
1 large tomato, peeled
  and chopped

1 bunch coriander, ground
1 tsp. ground hot pepper
  or 1 hot pepper, sliced
5 cups hot water
1 cup fresh peas
2½ cups rice, washed
¼ cup vegetable oil

After defrosting, cut duck into serving pieces. Season duck with salt and pepper to taste.

In a large frypan, brown duck in the ½ cup oil. Remove duck from pan. In the same oil brown the garlic, onion and tomato. Add coriander and peppers. Cook 2 minutes. Return duck to the pan and add water. Cook over moderate heat until almost done. Add the fresh peas and rice. Season and cook over high heat for 10 minutes. Reduce heat and simmer for about 15 minutes, or until rice is cooked and dry. 5 minutes before removing from the heat, add ½ cup oil and stir in gently. Serves 6.

CHICKEN WITH PORK ADOBO

PHILIPPINES

1 broiler, about 2 lbs.
2 lbs. pork (with
  considerable fat)
½ cup vinegar
4 cloves garlic

2 tbs. soy sauce
1 tsp. salt
¼ tsp. pepper
2 tbs. lard

Cut chicken into 6 or 8 serving pieces. Cut pork into 1 inch cubes.

Place chicken and pork into a saucepan and add vinegar, garlic, soy sauce, salt and pepper. Bring to a boil and simmer until meat is tender (about 45 minutes).

Remove meat and drain, reserving liquid. Saute meat in melted lard until well browned.

In a second saucepan, mash or grind the chicken liver and add liquid drained from meat. Heat until it begins to boil. Add the browned meat to the liquid and mix carefully to avoid breaking meat. Add salt and pepper to taste. Keep hot until ready to serve.

Serve with boiled rice. Serves 6 to 8.

HUNG MEN CHI CHICKEN

CHINA

Back in 1943, a number of Maryknoll Sisters were repatriated from Manchuria. One of the main topics among the Sisters returning home aboard the Gripsholm was food (probably sparked by the scarcity of edibles during their many years of house arrest in the Orient).

Sister M. de Lellis McKenna kept many of the recipes which were exchanged on that voyage. The following is one of them.

1 frying chicken (3-4 lbs.)	Fat for deep frying
Flour	2 eggs, well beaten
Salt	2 tbs. brown sugar
Pepper	1 cup boiling water
	2 tbs. soy sauce

Cut chicken into serving pieces. Mix flour, salt and pepper.

Roll chicken in flour mixture. Dip in beaten egg into which brown sugar has been added. Drop chicken into deep fat and fry to deep brown.

Leave a small amount of fat in frypan. Return chicken with boiling water and soy sauce and cook for 5 minutes. Cover and simmer until tender. Serves 4.

GUATEMALAN ROAST TURKEY

1 turkey, size for your family	½ lb. butter
1 chopped large onion	Bay leaves
2 tbs. mustard	Basil leaves
Salt and pepper	Juice of 15 oranges

Wash turkey and prick all over with fork. Rub in a mixture of salt and pepper and refrigerate overnight.

The following day rub in the mustard and refrigerate for another night.

On the third day, rub in butter and a large amount of chopped onion.

Place turkey in large roasting pan. Cover with crushed bay and basil leaves. Carefully pour orange juice over turkey. Roast in 250°F. oven according to standard roasting tables until well done. Baste at intervals to keep turkey moist.

CHICKEN CURRY

HAWAII

1 chicken (3-4 lbs.)	1 tbs. curry powder
Salt and pepper to taste	2 tbs. flour
2 tbs. butter	1 cup milk
1 clove garlic, mashed	2 cups coconut cream
1 tbs. chopped onion	1 tsp. salt

Cut chicken into serving pieces. Season with salt and pepper. Place in stew pot with few slices of onion and add just enough water to cover chicken. Cover tightly and simmer until meat is tender.

While chicken is simmering, put butter in top half of a double boiler, add mashed garlic and chopped onion. Saute for a few minutes, then add curry powder and continue to fry. Next add flour, stirring constantly. Slowly add milk.

Now remove from heat and insert this pan into bottom half of double boiler. Add coconut cream slowly. Then add salt. Cook until thick, stirring all the time.

Just before serving, add chicken with its juices to the curry sauce. Serve with rice. Pass a tray with small dishes containing quartered limes, chutney, pineapple pickle, chopped crisp bacon, chopped hard-boiled eggs, grated coconut, shredded dry fish and chopped coconut chips. Serves 4.

CHICKEN LUAU

HAWAII

1 cup fresh coconut
1 cup coconut milk
1 chicken (2-3 lbs.)
2 tsp. salt

1½ lbs. spinach or
  greens
3 tbs. butter

Grate the coconut. Heat the coconut milk, but do not boil. Combine both and set aside.

Cut chicken into serving pieces. Or bone and cut into 1½ inch cubes, if you prefer. Saute chicken in butter in frypan. When chicken is browned, squeeze coconut juice from grated coconut. Add coconut milk to frypan and simmer until chicken is tender.

Wash and drain spinach. Melt butter in a heavy saucepan, cover and steam for a few minutes until done.

When the chicken is tender, add the cooked spinach and stir to mix together. (Some prefer to add the coconut milk to the chicken; then pour some of the juice over the spinach and serve separately.) Serves 4.

PEKING DUCK

CHINA

1 duck, frozen
Salt and pepper to taste
Dark molasses

After defrosting in refrigerator, dry duck thoroughly and let stand for 6 hours at room temperature.

Rub inside and out with salt and pepper mixture, then rub outside of duck with dark molasses. Place duck on rack in roasting pan.

Roast in 350°F. oven for 2 hours or until skin is crisp.

Cut skin into serving pieces and place on one side of serving platter. Cut off meat and place on the other side of the platter. Serve with pancakes.

Pancakes for Peking Duck
Flour
Hot water
Vegetable oil

Mix flour with sufficient water to form a dough which can be kneaded to the right consistency to be rolled.

Form dough into balls half the size of an egg.

Take two dough balls and flatten with the palm of the hand. Brush one side of each flattened ball with the vegetable oil. Place the 2 oiled sides together, one atop the other, and roll out.

Put this double sheet of dough in a lightly greased frypan and cook first one side, then the other. Remove from frypan and carefully separate the two sheets, making two very thin pancakes. Steam until ready to serve.

To eat Peking Duck, spread Hoi Sin (or tomato catsup) on a pancake using a fresh scallion. Then wrap the scallion, a piece of skin and a piece of duck meat in the pancake and eat with the fingers. Serves 6.

BARBECUED CHICKEN

PHILIPPINES

Sister Edna Foster, who contributed this tasty recipe, writes that chicken prepared in this fashion is part of every fiesta. One taste and you'll want it at every one of your cookouts.

2 broiling chickens	*1 cup vinegar*
(3-4 lbs. each)	*2–4 cloves of garlic,*
2 cups soy sauce	*crushed*

Cut chickens up into serving pieces. Combine garlic, vinegar and soy sauce in a deep bowl, add chicken and allow to marinate overnight. Turn pieces several times so that chicken is well marinated.

Cook chicken over charcoal for an elegant flavor. It may also be fried in deep fat, if you prefer. Serves 8.

CHICKEN WITH SPINACH

HAWAII

1 stewing chicken
  (3-4 lbs.)
1 lb. spinach
1 qt. coconut cream

Cut chicken up into serving pieces. Put into saucepan with water, add salt and cook until tender.

Clean and boil spinach until tender. Drain and mash to a pulp.

Put chicken and spinach into a saucepan and cook gently for about 10 minutes. Add coconut cream and let simmer very gently for 5 more minutes (but never boil). Serves 4.

SWEET STUFFING FOR ROAST CHICKEN

ALBANIA

2 cups soft bread crumbs
½ cup butter
¼ cup currants
1 tbs. chicken broth

¼ cup raisins
½ cup chopped mixed
  nuts
½ cup sugar

Lightly brown the bread crumbs in butter. Add the currants, raisins, chopped nuts, sugar and chicken broth, one by one, mixing well. Toss the entire mixture lightly.

Fill a 3-to-4 pound roasting chicken with the stuffing and roast in a normal manner. Serves 4–6.

CHICKEN HIMALAYAN

PAKISTAN

1 roasting chicken
  (4 lbs.)
1 small onion
1 medium ginger root

2 tbs. black pepper
1 tsp. salt
1 cup yogurt
½ cup butter

Shred onion and ginger root together. If fresh ginger root is unavailable, substitute ⅛ tsp. of ground ginger. Mix with pepper, salt and yogurt, then pour over chicken. Pierce chicken all over with fork and rub mixture in. Soak for an hour or longer.

Melt butter in deep pan and cook chicken slowly (about 2 hours). Turn frequently. Chicken may be roasted if preferred.

ROAST CHICKEN
WITH ALMOND STUFFING

INDIA

1 roasting chicken (3-4 lbs.)	2 hard-boiled eggs
	1 lemon
Stuffing:	2 tbs. blanched almonds
4 small boiled potatoes	½ cup seedless raisins

Prepare chicken for roasting.

To prepare stuffing, dice potatoes and eggs, and sprinkle with lemon juice. Chop almonds. Mix almonds and raisins in potato mixture. Stuff in roasting chicken and proceed according to standard roasting time table. Serves 4–6.

CHICKEN PASTEL

PHILIPPINES

1 chicken (3-4 lbs.)	Salt and pepper to taste
1 can Vienna sausages	1 Spanish sausage (Chorizo de Bilbao)
1 cup canned peas, drained	Juice of 1 lemon
3 tbs. soy sauce	2 hard-boiled eggs
6 tbs. butter	5 cups cold water

Bone and cut chicken into small pieces. Place meat into bowl, adding lemon juice and soy sauce. Mix thoroughly and let stand about 15 minutes.

Put meat in saucepan with water, salt and pepper.

Simmer until the meat is tender. Let most of the liquid evaporate.

Slice Spanish sausage and saute with the cooked chicken in butter until brown. Remove from heat and place mixture in a Pyrex serving dish.

Slice Vienna sausages and hard-boiled eggs and arrange together with peas on top of meat in baking dish. Allow to cool.

Cover top with pie crust, press edges and bake in moderate oven (425°F) until crust turns brown. Serve hot. Serves 6.

CHICKEN WITH VEGETABLES AND ALMONDS

CHINA

This recipe comes to us from Mrs. Thomas Yang, the former Laureen Li. She was a student and is a long time friend of the Sisters.

½ lb. string beans	½ cup blanched almonds
3 tbs. vegetable oil	1 cup diced celery
1 tsp. salt	1 cup sliced celery cabbage
Dash of black pepper	
1 lb. cooked chicken, cut into slices, 1½ inches wide.	1 cup chicken bouillon
	2 tbs. cornstarch
¼ lb. fresh sliced mushrooms	2 tsp. soy sauce
	½ cup water

Precook string beans, cut into ½ inch pieces.

Heat together in a frypan the oil, salt and pepper. Add the sliced chicken, mushrooms, almonds, celery, celery cabbage and chicken bouillon. Cover and cook for 5 minutes. Add cooked string beans.

In a cup blend cornstarch, soy sauce and water. Add this mixture slowly to the ingredients in the frypan, stirring constantly until the liquid thickens and the mixture is very hot. Serve with boiled rice. Serves 6.

HAWAIIAN CHICKEN
MADE WITH COCONUT

The blend of coconut milk and pineapple gives this dish a real Hawaiian flavor. It's also called 2-Way Hawaiian Chicken as it is made both with and without curry powder.

1 frying chicken (2½-3 lbs.)	1¼ cups coconut milk (or 50/50 coconut milk and regular milk)
⅓ cup flour	1 cup pineapple chunks
1 tsp. salt	2 cups shredded coconut
¼ tsp. pepper	½ tsp. curry powder
¼ cup vegetable oil	

Remove skin from chicken and cut up into serving pie pieces. Dredge in flour mixed with salt and pepper. Saute in oil until lightly browned.

Blend remaining flour with coconut milk and ½ cup of pineapple syrup. Add to chicken, cover and simmer until chicken is tender.

Add shredded coconut and pineapple. About 15 minutes before serving add curry powder to half of chicken mixture.

Serve in divided dish, half with curry and half without. Serve with boiled rice. Serves 6.

CHINESE DUCK

HAWAII

1 large duck, frozen	4-6 slices canned pineapple
1 cup mushrooms	½ cup soy sauce
1 medium ginger root	2-3 cloves garlic
2 tbs. salad oil	2 tbs. butter

After defrosting, cut duck into serving pieces and marinate in a mixture of soy sauce, crushed garlic and ground ginger for several hours.

Place oil in frypan and fry duck until golden. Transfer to a casserole and add juice from the canned pineapple, sliced mushrooms and soy sauce. Cook until tender.

Fry pineapple slices in butter and serve with the duck. Serves 4.

PINEAPPLE CHICKEN

CHINA

1 chicken (4-6 lbs.)
1½ cups pineapple, diced
1 cup sliced mushrooms
1 cup bamboo shoots, sliced paper thin
1 cup sliced water chestnuts
Juice of ½ lemon
Pepper to taste

1 inch ginger root, finely chopped, or 2 tsp. ginger powder
1 tsp. sugar
1½ tsp. salt
1 tbs. soy sauce
1 tbs. cornstarch
1 cup water

Cut chicken into serving pieces. Fry in hot greased frypan for 10 minutes.

Add ginger, water chestnuts, bamboo shoots, mushrooms, lemon juice, water, soy sauce, sugar, salt and pepper. Add cornstarch to the ingredients in the frypan, stirring constantly until the liquid thickens. Then add pineapple and serve hot. Serves 6.

CHICKEN AND WALNUTS

CHINA

1 cup blanched walnuts
6 chopped mushrooms
2 cups diced chicken
3 tsp. soy sauce

3 tbs. flour
3 tbs. lard
1 tsp. sugar
1 tsp. salt

Roll chicken in flour and saute in melted lard for one minute. Cook while stirring frequently until chicken is golden brown. Add sugar, salt and soy sauce. Cook until chicken is done, stirring constantly. Stir in chopped mushrooms. Add walnuts. Serves 4.

Fish

SAFFRON FISH

CHINA

With the gold of the saffron for eye appeal, plus the delicate but compelling flavor of saffron, mace, ginger and lemon, here is a fish entree complete with sauce. No garnish is required.

1½ or 2 lbs. white fish
   (halibut, flounder or
   sole) sliced
2 tbs. butter
2 tbs. onion powder
1 tbs. Mei Yen season-
   ing powder
1 cup water
¼ tsp. ground ginger
½ tsp. black pepper

1/16 tsp. mace
½ tsp. salt
3 tbs. lemon juice
2 tbs. arrowroot
1 egg
Saffron, measured with
   the tip of a table knife,
   taking no more than
   ½ the size of a split
   pea

In a large heavy skillet, saute the onion powder slowly in butter for at least 5 minutes.

Wipe fish slices very dry and place in browned onion. Turn heat to low, cover skillet and simmer 10 minutes.

Place all other ingredients except water and saffron into a bowl and blend thoroughly.

Dissolve saffron in water and combine with the egg and seasonings mixture.

Pour mixture on and around the fish, raising each piece carefully with a wide spatula. Turn up heat until sauce begins to bubble. Reduce heat, cover skillet and simmer 10 minutes longer. By this time sauce should be smooth and creamy. Serve hot. Serves 6 to 8.

STUFFED CRABS

PHILIPPINES

6 crabs, boiled and
   flaked

6 crab shells
2 eggs, separated

2 tbs. chopped onion   1 tbs. salt
1 tbs. chopped tomato   Pinch of black pepper
6 tbs. cooking oil

In a skillet saute onion, crab meat and tomato in oil. Add seasonings.

Beat egg whites until stiff. In a separate bowl, beat egg yolks until thick and light in color. Fold yolks into whites, lightly and evenly.

Mix half of the egg mixture with the sauteed crab mixture. Fill each crab shell with the mixture. Then cover the tops with the remainder of the beaten eggs and fry in oil until brown. Serves 6.

BROILED MULLET

HAWAII

1 fresh mullet   1 cup chopped
¼ cup chopped   tomatoes
   scallions   ½ tsp. salt

Split the fish and remove the bones.

Mix the remaining ingredients and stuff the fish.

Wrap the mullet in corn husks or banana leaves and broil over charcoal for about 12 minutes on each side.

Open, serve with lemon and steamed rice. Serves 6.

PUNGENT FRIED FISH

AFRICA

6 white fish fillets   ½ tsp. saffron
Sauce   1 tsp. salt
1 red chili pepper   1 tbs. vinegar
⅛ tsp. cummin seed   Butter for frying

Mash or grind the chili pepper, cummin seed, saffron and salt, and moisten with a little vinegar. Rub this well into the fish and allow to stand for 5 to 10 minutes.

Pan fry in butter and serve hot. Usually served along with another dish such as a curried meat stew. Serves 6.

LOMI SALMON

HAWAII

5 cups flaked salted
  salmon
3 cups mashed fresh
  tomatoes

1 small bunch green
  onions or 2 large
  sliced onions
Ice

Soak salmon, preferably belly salmon, in cold water from 4 to 8 hours until soft. Drain, scale and flake into small pieces.

Skin tomatoes and mash to a pulp. Scrape or slice thinly the amount of onion desired.

Then *lomi-lomi* (work with hands) the salmon, tomato and onion together. When well *lomi-lomied,* add ice and serve. A little water may be added if a more watery consistency is desired, but usually the water from the ice is sufficient. Serves 12.

STUFFED FILLETS

PORTUGAL

2 lbs. fish fillets
Salt
Pepper
1 lemon
1 small glass white
  wine

White sauce
1 cup cooked shrimp
Bread crumbs
1 egg
½ cup vegetable oil

Cut fillets into rectangles. Season with salt and pepper. Add a few drops lemon juice and the wine. Marinate for 1 hour.

Add shrimp to thick white sauce and allow to get cold.

Stuff fillets with shrimp sauce, roll in bread crumbs, then in beaten egg, and again in crumbs.

Fry in oil, drain and serve with tomato sauce. Serves 6.

VELVET FISH BALLS

CHINA

½ cup fish flesh (cod, halibut or tuna)
1 cup cold water
¼ tsp. salt

1 egg white
3 slices macerated ginger

Chop fish very finely. Add water gradually. Then add salt and the egg white, slightly beaten. Bean curd may also be added, if desired.

To cook, drop into boiling water.

SHRIMP SANDWICH

CHINA

8 slices bread, without crust, or 4 thick slices slit bookwise

1 cup chopped canned or fresh shrimp
½ tbs. ginger
2 tbs. soy sauce

Mix together shrimp, ginger and soy sauce.

Fill sandwiches with mixture and pinch edges to hold together.

Fry in deep fat and serve hot. A delicious luncheon recipe. Serves 4.

STEAMED SPICED FISH

LAOS

4 fish fillets from an oily fish such as shad or mackerel
1 lb. fish roe

½ tsp. salt
¼ tsp. cayenne pepper
4 spring onions, chopped fine

Cut fillets into 1-inch pieces. Blend well with roe, salt, pepper and onions. Divide mixture into quarters and wrap each portion in aluminum foil.

Steam above gently boiling water in a steamer for 45 minutes.

Serve with steamed rice. Serves 4.

SWEET AND SOUR FISH

CHINA

6 firm whole whitefish
Sauce
2 cups water
½ cup vinegar
¼ cup sugar
2 tbs. soy sauce

1 tbs. ginger root, sliced thin
5 green onions, chopped
2 tbs. cornstarch
Pepper to taste

Clean the fish, removing the scales and fins but not the head. Dry fish and brown in deep fat. When browned, place on an oven-proof platter and keep warm in the oven. If fish is not thoroughly cooked inside, raise oven temperature so as to finish cooking (about 350°F).

To prepare the sauce, boil the water. Mix the vinegar and cornstarch together, then add slowly to the water. Add the remaining ingredients, with the onions last, and cook until the cornstarch is cooked.

Pour the sauce over the fish and serve garnished with parsley. Serves 6.

TUNA CHOP SUEY

HAWAII

The Chinese-Hawaiians serve fish frequently and in a variety of forms. This dish is especially good prepared with water-packed tuna.

1 sliced onion
2 cups sliced celery
2 tbs. shortening
½ tsp. salt
Dash of pepper

1½ cups hot water
½ lb. bean sprouts
½ cup sliced mushrooms
1 7-oz. can tuna, flaked

2 sliced green onions
2 tbs. cornstarch
2 tbs. water

1 tbs. soy sauce
1 tbs. sugar

Cook onion and celery in melted shortening. Add seasonings and hot water. Simmer for 3 minutes.

Add bean sprouts, mushrooms, tuna and green onions. Combine remaining ingredients and add to the vegetable mixture. Cook until sauce thickens. Serve hot over crisp noodles. Serves 4.

COCONUT FISH

HAWAII

The girls at St. Anthony's School prepared this dish at a picnic on a Maui beach, using one coconut per person. Sister Celestine Naes sent us the recipe.

6 green coconuts
6 tbs. chopped
    scallions

6 tbs. chopped salt pork
    or lard
6 cups boned white
    fish

Cut off the top of each coconut, sometimes called "spoon" coconuts because their meat is soft enough to be spooned out. Retain the coconut juice.

Fill each coconut with 1 tbs. scallions, 1 tbs. salt pork and 1 cup fish. Pour in coconut juice to 1-inch below the top.

Replace the tops, wrap the coconuts in aluminum foil and place into a charcoal fire, standing them carefully so as not to tip. Allow to cook for about 45 minutes, or until the fish is cooked through.

Chicken may also be fixed the same way, but it is necessary to parboil the chicken for about 40 minutes before filling the coconuts (or else cook the coconuts in charcoal for a much longer period).

To prepare indoors, bake in a 350°F oven for about 40 minutes.

Serve hot with plenty of steamed rice. Serves 6.

TEMPURA

JAPAN

½ oz. sake or sherry
2½ cups water
2 tbs. sugar
½ cup soy sauce
1 egg
½ cup flour
10 small shrimp

5 scallops
2 lobster tails
10 mushroom caps
5 green peppers
Vegetable oil
Grated ginger
Grated radish

First prepare shrimp and lobster tails. Remove the head and shell from shrimp, leaving tail. Devein and wash in cold water. Put lobster tails into rapidly boiling water to harden meat. Remove lobster meat from shell carefully. Then cut lobster meat into bite-sized pieces.

To prepare batter, beat egg in a small bowl. Add flour and ½ cup of water and blend lightly.

To cook, dip seafood, mushrooms and quartered peppers into batter and deep fry in oil until golden brown.

As *tempura* is a style of cooking, assorted vegetables such as carrots, sweet potatoes, asparagus, string beans, etc., can also be dipped and fried.

Serve with the following *tare* sauce. To prepare, add sugar, soy sauce to 2 cups boiling water. Allow to cool slightly, then add sake and mix well. Put *tare* sauce in individual bowls, making a small mound of grated radish and ginger in the center of each bowl. Dip seafood and vegetables into *tare* before eating. Serves 5.

FISH CURRY

PAKISTAN

1 cup yogurt
2 tsp. lemon juice
¼ tsp. powdered
    coriander
1 tsp. cayenne pepper

1 tsp. powdered ginger
¼ tsp. curry powder
1 tsp. oregano
½ cup chopped onion
4 fish fillets

½ cup vegetable oil   *⅛ tsp. cummin seeds*

Thoroughly blend all ingredients except fish, oil and cummin seeds in an electric blender or food mill.

Cut fish fillets in half. Roll each half and arrange in a shallow baking dish.

Mix oil and cummin seeds in a skillet, and heat until dark brown. Add the blended ingredients and brown, stirring constantly. Pour mixture over fish and bake 30 minutes at 350°F. Serves 8.

SHRIMP ROLLS

CHINA

*1 lb. cooked fresh
    shrimp
¼ lb. bacon
1 lemon
1 small piece ginger,
    chopped fine*

*2 egg whites
1½ cups water
½ tsp. sugar
2 tsp. cornstarch
2 tsp. soy sauce
Salt and pepper to taste*

Shell and devein fish, then wash in clean cold water.

Take a piece of bacon and cut it as long as each shrimp. Dip a clean knife into the egg whites and "butter" each shrimp. Then place a piece of bacon on each "buttered" shrimp and roll into a little roll, fastening with a toothpick.

Fry shrimp rolls and ginger together in a hot greased frypan for 5 minutes. Add the lemon juice, then thicken the gravy with cornstarch and water.

Season with soy sauce, sugar, pepper and salt. Serves 4 to 6.

STEAMED MULLET

HAWAII

Mullet is a native Hawaiian fish, somewhat similar to trout. This dish can be prepared with any similar fish, or with fillets of any white fish.

1½ lbs. mullet
4 slices lemon
4 slices onion
4 slices tomato

1 medium carrot,
  shredded
½-inch fresh ginger,
  grated
2 tbs. soy sauce

Clean fish and place on an oven-proof platter. Arrange the slices of lemon, onion and tomato over the fish.

Mix the grated ginger and soy sauce together and brush or drizzle over the fish. Shred the carrot and arrange over all.

Place the oven dish into a larger baking pan. Fill the pan with boiling water to just below the rim of the oven platter. Cover the pan and steam for about 45 minutes, adding water if necessary. Serve with rice. Serves 4.

ESCABECHENG APAHAP

PHILIPPINES

1 medium apahap or
  sea bass
4 pieces tokua or
  rice cake
2 cloves garlic
1 cup water
Several mushrooms

1 cup vinegar
½ cup sugar
1 red pepper
2 tbs. sifted flour
6 slices ginger root
2 tbs. cooking oil

Clean fish and rub with salt to taste.

Cut ginger and garlic in diagonal strips. Dice rice cakes.

Mix vinegar, sugar and salt until an agreeable sweet-sour taste is obtained. Cut pepper into quarters.

In a skillet, heat oil and pan fry fish with rice cakes until almost done. Set aside.

In the same oil, saute onions, ginger and garlic. Add vinegar mixture. When this comes to a boil, add fried fish, rice cakes, mushrooms and pepper. Cover and continue to cook for 5 minutes. When almost done, add flour which has been mixed with 1 cup hot water. Stir gently until thick. Serve hot. Serves 4.

DEEP FRIED PRAWNS ON TOAST

SOUTH CHINA

A crusty, delicious bite—anywhere. Sent by Sister Mary Rosalia Kettl, who says to try it with shrimp, crayfish or any similar variety of local fish.

1 lb. prawns	2 eggs
5 tbs. flour	Water, as needed
½ lb. bread	Salt and pepper to taste

Unshell the prawns, but not entirely. Leave the tail on each to hold it together. Split and open prawn from top to tail, wash and dry with a cloth.

Sprinkle prawn with pepper and salt and allow to stand for 10 minutes.

Make a paste with the flour, eggs and a little water. Cut bread slices into halves.

Dip the entire prawn into the paste and lay it flat on a half piece of bread.

Deep fry the combination until golden. Serves 4.

CURRIED SHRIMP

HAWAII

2 tbs. butter	½ cup milk
1 tbs. minced onion	1 cup cream
1 clove garlic, whole	2 tbs. chutney
1½ tbs. flour	2 tbs. lemon juice
2 tsp. curry powder	2½ cups fresh or
Salt and pepper to taste	canned shrimp

Saute onion and garlic gently in butter for 5 minutes. Discard garlic and add flour and curry powder to the onion and butter. Blend smooth, then stir in milk and cream.

Cook over medium heat, stirring until smoothly thickened. Add chutney, lemon juice and shrimp. Heat thoroughly, season to taste and serve on hot cooked rice with chutney and any or all of the following accompaniments: crisp bacon, finely chopped hard-boiled eggs, shredded fresh coconut, small pickled onions, chopped peanuts. Serves 6.

PRAWNS ESPANOL

GUATEMALA

Prawns bring a welcome change from the usual fish meal—especially if they are prepared after this exotic Latin recipe.

3 tbs. olive oil	¼ tsp. celery seed
4 tbs. green peppers	¼ bay leaf
1 small can tomatoes	⅛ tsp. garlic powder
1 tsp. onion powder	3 tbs. whole parsley
1 cup hot tomato sauce	¼ tsp. salt
½ tsp. basil	2 lbs. prawns
⅛ tsp. rosemary	3 beef bouillon cubes
⅛ tsp. oregano	1 cup rice

In a saucepan, saute the onion powder and peppers in oil. Do not scorch. Mash the tomatoes and add the hot tomato sauce, garlic powder, crushed rosemary, basil and oregano. Next add celery seed, bay leaf, parsley and salt. Add bouillon cubes and simmer 2 hours. Add 2 lbs. precooked prawns, just before serving over steamed rice. Serves 6 to 8.

SALMON GOHAN

JAPAN

2 cups rice	1 tbs. salad oil
2½ cups water	1 small onion
1 tbs. sake or cooking sherry	1 can small red salmon
1 tsp. chopped ginger	2 tbs. sake or cooking sherry
1 tsp. salt	2 tbs. sugar

Few drops red food
  coloring
1 cup parboiled peas

Shredded pickled ginger
  or pickled beets

Wash rice and drain. Add the required amount of water and let stand for 45 minutes.

Drain salmon and add liquid to rice water. Add sake, chopped ginger and salt to rice and cook in usual manner.

Flake salmon and remove bones and skin.

Heat oil in pan and saute onions 5 minutes. Add flaked salmon, sake, sugar, salt and food coloring. Stir and cook 5 minutes or until liquid has evaporated.

When rice is cooked, remove to a bowl. Add salmon mixture and stir lightly.

Sprinkle with peas, garnish with pickled beets. Serves 4.

SHRIMP CURRY

HAWAII

On Mother Mary Joseph's first visit to the Maryknoll Sisters in Hawaii, she was served Shrimp Curry. She obtained the recipe and included it in her personal cookbook.

3 coconuts
3 tbs. hot water
1½ cups coconut milk
1½ cups milk
6 tbs. flour
1 lb. fresh or canned
  shrimp

1 tsp. ginger juice, or
  2 tsp. ginger powder
1 tsp. curry powder
1½ tsp. lemon juice
1½ tsp. finely chopped
  onion
Salt to taste

Grate coconut meat. Add coconut milk and hot water to grated coconut meat and allow to stand 15 minutes. Strain through 2 thicknesses of cheese cloth. Squeeze out as much juice as possible. Discard juice and reserve coconut.

Shell and devein shrimp and wash in cold water. Drain and set aside.

In a skillet, melt butter and add chopped onion and flour.

Cook slowly until it forms a smooth paste. Then add strained coconut and milk. Add shrimp and seasonings and heat slowly for ½ hour.

Serve on a platter, surrounded by rice and topped with shredded coconut. Serves 6.

SHRIMP AND MUSHROOMS

CHINA

4 tbs. vegetable oil	1 cup water
3 lbs. fresh shrimp	Slices of ginger root,
1 cup mushrooms	to taste
1 tbs. cornstarch	3 tsp. sugar

Shell and devein shrimp, wash clean in cold water to which salt and pepper have been added. Drain.

In a large skillet, heat oil and add sliced ginger. Saute shrimp in oil until they are pink, then drain off oil. Set shrimp aside.

In the same pan, braise mushrooms for 3 minutes, turning constantly. Return shrimp to pan and mix well.

To prepare sauce, boil together in a separate pan the cornstarch, sugar and water. Serve over shrimp and mushrooms. Serves 8.

FRIED FISH

KOREA

6 slices fish, ¼-inch thick	1½ tbs. cooking oil
	1 tbs. sesame oil
2 tbs. white sesame seed, browned and pulverized	⅓ cup finely chopped green onions with tops
	Pinch black pepper
6 tbs. soy sauce	

Use a fish with firm flesh and very few bones.

Dip the fish in the mixture of soy sauce, sesame oil, sesame seeds, pepper and onions.

In a frypan, heat oil and fry fish until thoroughly cooked. May be served with red pepper sauce. Serves 4.

Hot pepper sauce

2 tsp. sesame oil
¼ tsp. ground red pepper
1 tsp. sugar
1 tsp. white sesame seed, browned and pulverized

2 tbs. green onion with tops, chopped
1 clove finely chopped garlic
2 tsp. ginger root, finely chopped
¼ cup soy sauce

Combine ingredients, pour over browned fish and continue to simmer for 2 minutes. Serve hot, garnished with finely chopped onion and pulverized sesame seeds.

FU YUN TAN

CHINA

A crab-egg delight from Sister Margaret Marie Jung.

6 eggs
½ tsp. salt
Pepper to taste

⅛ cup chopped onion, if desired
8 oz. crab meat
½ cup water

Crack eggs into a medium-sized bowl, add water, salt and pepper. Beat gently with a fork or chopsticks until small bubbles appear.

Add the crab meat to the egg mixture, small quantities at a time, stirring gently while adding. Leave crab meat in small lumps. The batter is now ready for frying.

Use a hot, well greased frypan. If onions are used, brown them first, then add the egg mixture to them.

Let this cook for 1 minute over medium heat. Then, with a spatula, gently scrape back the cooked egg and let the uncooked batter run onto the pan surface. Keep scraping until all the batter is done.

Garnish by placing a few stalks of Chinese mustard greens around the eggs. Serves 4.

TUNA CHOW MEIN

HAWAII

1 Bermuda onion, diced	*1 stalk celery, diced*
1 small can mushrooms	*Soy sauce to taste*
2 cans cream of	*1 can bamboo shoots*
mushroom soup	*(optional)*
2 7-oz. cans water	*Frenched green beans*
packed tuna	*(optional as a filler)*

In a large skillet, fry celery, onions and mushrooms in butter. Add bamboo shoots and green beans, browning slightly. Add tuna and cook 5 minutes.

Add mushroom soup, season to taste with soy sauce, salt and pepper.

Transfer mixture to the top half of a double boiler and heat until very hot. Serve over rice or noodles. Serves 6.

Stews

KANAKA STEW

HAWAII

1½ lbs. stew meat or
  short ribs
1 cup chopped onions
2 tbs. butter

½ tsp. salt
¾ cup fresh or canned
  poi

Melt butter in a deep saucepan and brown meat. Add enough water to cover and simmer for about 3 hours or until meat is tender.

An hour before stew is cooked add salt.

About 15 minutes before serving add the poi and allow to heat thoroughly.

Serve with rice. Serves 6.

AFRICAN STEW

AFRICA

This unusual recipe uses almost any kind of meat that is available to Africans. Beef is used when a special day requires it. The recipe was sent to us by Sister Patricia Hafey.

1 lb. stew meat
3 potatoes, cubed
3 small onions
4 small green bananas

1 tbs. butter
1½ cups coconut
1 cup boiling water
Salt to taste

Cut the meat into bite-sized pieces. Put into a soup pot and cover with water.

Peel the bananas, remove the seed line, cut up and wash well. Add to the meat. Add the chopped onions.

Cook all together until the meat is tender and the bananas are mushy. Remove the meat. Strain the gravy, pushing the pulp of the bananas and onions through the strainer.

Return the meat to the gravy, add the cubed potatoes.

Prepare coconut milk by pouring 1 cup boiling water over the grated coconut, allowing it to soak for 15 minutes, then straining and squeezing it through a clean cloth. Add this milk to the mixture.

Cook gently until potatoes are cooked. When potatoes are not available, this dish is served with rice which has been cooked separately, or with a local cornmeal mush (ugali) made from fresh ground corn. Serves 4.

BEEF SUKIYAKI

JAPAN

2 lbs. fillet of beef thinly
   sliced
2 onions
6 scallions or 10
   Japanese leeks
2 tbs. olive oil or beef
   suet
Small bunch mitsuba
   (marsh parsley)
6 fresh mushrooms

¼ cup sugar
½ cup soy sauce
2 whole bamboo
   shoots, canned
½ cup soup stock
1 tbs. sake or sherry
4 stalks celery
2 cakes tofu (bean curd)

Cut the onions into slices. Slice the scallions (or leeks) into 2-inch lengths. Cut the celery into diagonal slices. Slice the bamboo shoots into thin strips. Finally, cut the *tofu* (bean curd) into thirds and the mushrooms into lengthwise slices. Set aside.

Prepare the special broth called *warishita* by boiling soy sauce, the soup stock, sugar and sake. Set aside.

Heat olive oil in a large, heavy skillet. Add a small quantity of meat, which has been cut crossgrained into thin slices, and cook lightly. Pour *warishita* broth over the meat and bring to a boil. Add gradually in small quantities the onions, scallions and celery. Cover and cook for 5 minutes over low heat.

Add the remaining sauce, *tofu*, bamboo shoots, *mitsuba*

(optional) and mushrooms. Cook uncovered for 3 minutes. It is important not to overcook.

In traditional Japanese style, sukiyaki may be served with a lightly beaten egg in individual bowls. The stew is dipped into the beaten egg before eating. Serves 5 to 6.

VEGETABLE STEW

ECUADOR

2 tbs. oil
2 chopped onions
2 cloves garlic, chopped
½ cup tomato sauce
½ cup water
1 cup corn kernels
1 cup green peas

1 tsp. salt
½ tsp. pepper
4 potatoes, peeled and quartered
2 cups pumpkin puree
¾ cup American cheese grated
1 cup milk

Saute onions and garlic in a saucepan with the oil.

Stirring frequently, add tomato sauce, water, corn, peas, salt and pepper. Cover and cook over low flame for 10 minutes.

Add potatoes and pumpkin, again cover and cook for 20 minutes longer. Add cheese and milk, mix well and cook for another 5 minutes.

Serve with noodles or rice. Serves 6.

MEAT STEW

ETHIOPIA

½ lb. butter
2 cups minced onions
1 cup water
2 lbs. boneless lamb (beef or veal)

1 tsp. salt
1 tsp. black pepper
1 tbs. cornstarch
¼ cup cold water

Melt half of the butter in a heavy saucepan. Add onions

and cook over medium heat until they are soft. Mix in remaining butter and 1 cup water. Cook uncovered for 5 minutes.

Add the meat (which has been cut into bite-sized pieces) and the seasonings, cover pan and simmer mixture for 1½ hours.

Blend 1 tbs. cornstarch with ¼ cup of cold water. Add this mixture to the simmering stew to thicken the sauce and continue cooking for 5 minutes. Serve over cooked rice or noodles. Serves 6 to 8.

SCALLOP AND SHRIMP STEW

CHILE

1 lb. scallops, washed
1 lb. shrimp shelled and
   deveined
½ cup water
½ cup white wine
1½ cups bread crumbs
1 cup milk
½ lb. butter
2 sliced onions

1 tbs. paprika
1 cup cream
2 tsp. salt
½ tsp. black pepper
½ tsp. oregano
4 hard-boiled eggs
½ cup grated Parmesan
   cheese

Bring the scallops, shrimp and wine to a boil in a saucepan. Cook over low heat for 5 minutes, until shrimp are pink. Strain, reserving stock.

Chop the seafood coarsely, with the exception of 2 or 3 scallops and shrimp.

Soak the bread crumbs in milk and melt the butter in the saucepan. Add onions and paprika. Saute 10 minutes, stirring frequently.

Squeeze the excess milk from the bread and discard the milk. Combine the soaked bread crumbs with the onions and add the reserved stock. Mix well.

Combine the chopped seafood, cream, salt, pepper and oregano (⅛ tsp. chili powder may be substituted).

Stirring frequently, cook over low heat for 10 minutes. Place in casserole and garnish with hard-boiled eggs cut in wedges and the reserved scallops and shrimp. Sprinkle with Parmesan cheese, dot with butter and bake in preheated oven (400°F) for 20 minutes (or until golden brown). Serves 6.

CHOW MEIN, CANTONESE STYLE

CHINA

1 lb. noodles	1 cup bamboo shoots,
1 lb. pork, sliced thin	sliced thin
½ lb. fresh mushrooms,	2 cups meat broth
sliced thin	2 eggs
1 cup bean sprouts	1 tbs. soy sauce
2 tbs. salt	Pepper to taste
1 tbs. butter	

Drop raw noodles into a pot of boiling water to which salt has been added. Cook for 10 minutes. Drain noodles in a colander and run cold water over them to remove the starch. Drain well, spread in a large buttered baking pan, and dry in a warm oven.

In a saucepan, fry sliced pork with a little butter, add soy sauce and cook until a golden brown. (Chicken may be used with pork for flavor.) Add the mushrooms, bamboo shoots, bean sprouts and 1½ cups of meat broth. Cook 5 minutes and season with salt and pepper.

Beat the eggs slightly and fry in a greased pan in thin sheets like pancakes, but much thinner. Remove from pan when cooked, roll into a tube and slice into thin strips.

Remove noodles from the oven and fry in a hot greased pan for 3 minutes. Add ½ cup meat broth to the noodles, stirring constantly. Remove from pan and spread out on a large platter. Pour the meat mixture over the noodles. Garnish with the shredded egg and parsley. Serve hot. Serves 6.

ESTOFADO DE SAN JUAN

CHILE

A traditional meal served in Chile on June 24th, the fiesta of St. John the Baptist. It was sent to us by Sister Genevieve Reinhardt, who explained that it is difficult to give precise measurements as this dish is usually prepared and enjoyed in great quantities.

Poultry meat, chicken or turkey	Garlic and oregano to taste
Pork rind and some pork fat	White wine or red vinegar
Pieces of lean pork with bone	Onion cut into quarters
Dried cherries	Sausages

In a deep pan place a layer of onions, then pieces of pork rind, another layer of onions, then pieces of lean pork, a third layer of onions, then topped with the poultry meat cut into serving pieces and the sausages.

Sprinkle the condiments, both the dried cherries and the liquids, evenly over the surface. Cover well and steam for 2 or 3 hours, or until tender. Three pounds of meat serve 4 people.

SINIGAND NA CARNE

PHILIPPINES

1½ lbs. beef chuck with bone	Salt to taste
1 lb. pork slices	Bunch spinach, kale or mustard greens
½ medium onion, sliced	3 sliced tomatoes
5 limes or lemons	1 bunch string beans
2 medium radishes cut into large slices	

Simmer pork and beef in a large kettle with enough water

or rice washings to cover. Add sliced tomatoes, onion and salt. Squeeze the limes or lemons for their juice, which is added to the mixture. Boil and add additional water as needed. Add radishes.

When almost cooked, add string beans and either spinach, kale or mustard greens. Season with salt to taste. Serve hot with soy sauce and lemon juice. Serves 4.

Rice and Noodles

ARABIAN CASSEROLE

YEMEN

1 cup ground fenugreek
   seeds
3 cups water
½ tsp. bicarbonate of
   soda
1 lb. cooked ground beef
2 cups cooked rice

1½ cups tomato juice
8 tbs. leek juice or
   4 tbs. onion juice
1 tsp. salt
½ tsp. pepper
1 tbs. chopped mint

Obtain fenugreek seeds in an Oriental food store or store specializing in spices. Soak seeds in 3 cups water with bicarbonate of soda overnight. Drain, roll seeds to soften.

Mix seeds with cooked ground meat, cooked rice, tomato juice, leek juice, salt, pepper and mint.

Place in greased casserole dish and cook in moderate oven (350°F.) for thirty minutes. Serve hot. Serves 6.

ARROZ A LA FILIPINA

PHILIPPINES

½ cup boiled sticky rice
   (malagkit)
½ cup boiled rice
1 small chicken
3 cloves garlic, chopped
1 sliced small onion
Paprika strips to taste
Salt and pepper to taste

3 ripe medium tomatoes,
   sliced
3 medium green peppers
1 small pkg. raisins
1 hard-boiled egg
3 tbs. lard

Cut chicken into small pieces. In a large frypan, saute onion, garlic, tomatoes and chicken. Add salt and pepper to taste. Cook covered until chicken is brown. Add water and cook until tender. Add sliced green peppers and cook for a few minutes more.

Add strips of paprika for coloring. Then add the boiled sticky rice and raisins. Continue cooking over low heat until all the ingredients are tender.

Garnish with sliced hard-boiled egg and with green and red pepper slices. Serves 4.

SALMON GOHAN

JAPAN

2 cups uncooked rice
2½ cups water
1 tbs. sake or cooking
　sherry
1 tsp. chopped ginger
1 tsp. salt
1 tbs. salad oil
1 chopped small onion
1 small can red salmon

2 tbs. sake or cooking
　sherry
2 tbs. sugar
½ tsp. salt
2-4 drops red food color
½ cup par-boiled peas
Shredded beni shoga
　(pickled ginger) or use
　red pickled beets

Wash rice thoroughly and drain. Place in a large frypan, add the measured amount of water and let stand for 45 minutes. Drain liquid from canned salmon into the rice. Add 1 tbs. sake, chopped ginger and salt to the rice and cook until tender.

Flake salmon, removing bones and skin. In another pan, heat salad oil. Add onion and saute for 5 minutes. Add flaked salmon, sake, sugar, salt and food color. Stir and cook 5 minutes or until liquid has disappeared.

When rice is cooked, transfer to a bowl. Add salmon mixture and stir lightly. Sprinkle with peas and garnish with beni shoga. Serves 4.

NOODLES

KOREA

1 lb. fine noodles   2 tsp. salt
3 pints boiling water

Add salt and noodles to water and boil from 8 to 10 minutes, stirring constantly. Drain noodles in colander and rinse with cold water. Drain and place noodles in individual soup bowls. Garnish with ground cooked meat, narrow strips of fried egg yolks and whites, and finely chopped green onions. Pour hot soup over noodles and serve.

In Korea, noodles are frequently served cold in warm weather. The soup may be chilled with pieces of ice, the fat skimmed, and the cold soup poured over the cold noodles.

STICKY RICE

THAILAND

In Bangkok, most of the population are Chinese or a mixture of Chinese and other eastern peoples. The food, therefore, is a mixture of Chinese, Vietnamese and Thai dishes. In the north, however, most of the people are pure Thai and eat traditional Thai foods. One is Sticky Rice, used in Thailand much as we use bread. The following recipe was contributed by Sister M. Emmanuel Satsawang.

½ cup rice per person
  to be served
Water

Soak rice in cold water in a Pyrex dish. Soak for 3–4 hours. Decant and discard liquid.

Set Pyrex dish containing rice in a large soup pot into which an inch of water has been added. Cover larger vessel, turn heat to simmer and allow steam from bottom pot to cook rice in Pyrex dish.

How to serve:

Sticky Rice can be served with a special Thai sauce. Although not available outside the Orient, it may be imitated by making a paste of chopped boiled shrimp and chopped hot chili peppers.

Another way to serve Sticky Rice is with Fish Soy, a rather salty, tasty sauce available in most Oriental food stores. It does not have the hot taste of the shrimp paste and chili.

TAMBI

AFRICA

Sister Margaret Hart sent us this recipe, popular among the Moslems during their fasting season.

1 cup sugar
2 tbs. cooking oil
¼ tsp. cardamom

1 pkg. vermicelli or fine noodles

Cook the noodles in boiling water until soft, then drain. In a large skillet heat the oil. Add the sugar, stirring continually until the sugar begins to brown.

Add the cooked noodles to the carmelized sugar and oil mixture and stir well. Cook for about 10 minutes, turning frequently.

When all the noodles are well coated and the sugar mixture is cooked into them, turn the noodles out onto a slightly oiled platter. Allow to cool before serving. Serves 4.

CHINESE-HAWAIIAN FRIED RICE

HAWAII

1 cup uncooked rice
½ cup diced pork,
   browned in fat
½ cup fried whole
   peanuts
½ cup finely chopped
   onions
½ cup sliced cooked
   mushrooms
1 tsp. soy sauce
4 well beaten eggs
Salt and pepper to taste
2 tbs. fat or salad oil

Boil rice until cooked, but not soft. Drain, fluff and allow to cool for about an hour.

Melt fat in large frypan. Add rice and saute for ½ hour, stirring often so rice will brown evenly.

When rice is well browned, add browned pork, fried peanuts, onions, mushrooms, soy sauce, salt and pepper. Saute for 1 minute, stirring to mix ingredients. Add 4 well beaten eggs, stirring constantly until eggs are well cooked.

Serve hot. Serves 5 to 6.

YELLOW RICE

SOUTH AFRICA

1 cup uncooked rice
2 cups boiling water
1 tbs. butter
½ cup seedless raisins
½ cup brown sugar
1½ tsp. turmeric
1½ tsp. salt

Wash rice and place with remaining ingredients into a saucepan with boiling water. Cover and bring quickly back to a boil, stirring with fork. Reduce heat and cook about 25 minutes, or until rice is tender. Serves 6.

ROYAL RICE

CAMBODIA

2 chicken legs, uncooked
½ lb. lean pork
4 shrimps, shelled and
  deveined
20 scallions
¾ cup lard or fat
3 cups cooked rice
Pinch of fennel seed or
  fennel sprigs
2 tbs. vinegar

2 eggs, slightly beaten
1½ cups medium white
  sauce
⅛ tsp. Chinese five-
  spice essence
2 tbs. powdered sugar
Dash of salt
Dash of pepper
2 tbs. pimiento strips
Juice of 1 lemon

Wash and dice chicken, pork and shrimp. Brown scallions in fat in skillet. Add meat and shrimp and saute for 30 minutes. Mix in cooked rice. Add fennel, sugar, vinegar, white sauce, five-spice essence, salt and pepper. Heat a few minutes to blend flavors.

Pour eggs into a greased skillet and heat until almost firm, then turn over. Remove eggs from heat and cut into ¼ inch strips and add to mixture. Transfer mixture to serving dish and garnish with pimientos and additional fennel. Sprinkle with lemon juice. Serves 4.

CHINESE RICE

When rice is cooked properly in China, every grain stands by itself. To prepare in this manner, first wash the rice clean. Place in a saucepan with sufficient water to measure 1 inch above the rice surface.

Heat to a boil, then turn heat down low, cover and simmer until rice is cooked dry. Do not open lid during the cooking. Fluff and serve.

SAIMIN

JAPAN

1 lb. macaroni	1 bunch green onions
1 large can mushrooms	5 slices bacon, chopped
1 can tuna	Soy sauce to taste

Cook macaroni. Cut onions into ½ inch pieces and the tops into 1 inch pieces. Fry together the chopped bacon and the white part of the onions. Add the mushrooms, ¼ cup soy sauce and ¼ cup of juice from the mushrooms. Cover and steam for 5 minutes. Add grated onions, tuna, macaroni, more soy sauce and mushroom juice, if needed. Steam covered over low heat for 20 minutes. Serve in bowls with a crisp green salad. Serves 8.

GUATEMALAN FRIED RICE

2 tbs. shortening	2 tbs. peas
2 cups uncooked rice	2 tbs. chopped green
1 small chopped onion	beans
1 clove garlic	½ finely chopped carrot
1 tomato, chopped	¼ chopped green pepper
1 tsp. salt	3 cups water

Wash rice thoroughly and let dry.

Heat shortening in large frypan. Add rice and saute until just brown, stirring constantly. Add onion and tomato. Cook for 2 minutes. Add water, salt and all other ingredients, stir, cover and bring to a boil. Then lower heat and simmer for 45 minutes, or until all ingredients are cooked.

Serve hot and with a fork, not a spoon. Serves 2.

CHINESE-HAWAIIAN FRIED NOODLES

HAWAII

Sister Madeline McHugh picked up this delicious dish in Hawaii. It's easy to prepare and very tasty. Try serving it with chopsticks and watch the fun.

1½ lbs. fine noodles
⅓ cup cooking oil
½ lb. pork cut in
   thin slices
½ lb. mushrooms,
   sliced

1 can bean sprouts
2 tbs. soy sauce
2 cups meat stock
3 or 4 green onions,
   chopped
⅓ cup cornstarch

Cook the noodles in boiling salted water for about 8 minutes. Rinse in cold water, drain, spread in a shallow dish and chill for several hours.

Brown the thin strips of pork in a little of the oil. Add the sliced mushrooms and cook 4 minutes. Add the meat stock and soy sauce and cook until mushrooms and pork are tender.

Mix the cornstarch with a little cold water and use to thicken the meat gravy. When cooked, add the bean sprouts and some of the chopped scallions.

In the meantime, heat the remaining oil in a skillet. Add the chilled noodles, pushing down in the skillet to form a "cake" of noodles. Do not stir. When browned on one side, turn and brown on the other.

To serve, "unmold" the noodles onto a serving platter, pour the pork mixture over it and garnish with the rest of the scallions.

Additional soy sauce may be served with this dish. Some cooks place a clove of garlic and a piece of ginger in the pan while frying the pork, removing them before adding the rest of the ingredients. Serves 4.

ARROZ TAPADA

BOLIVIA

2 tbs. olive oil
2 cloves crushed garlic
3 cups water
2 cups uncooked rice
2 tbs. shortening
½ cup chopped onion
2 sliced hard-boiled eggs

2 small tomatoes,
  chopped
1 cup ground meat
Salt and pepper to taste
½ cup seedless raisins
1 tbs. coarsely chopped
  parsley

In a saucepan, heat the oil, half the garlic and a dash of salt. Add water and bring to a boil. Add the rice, reduce the heat and simmer until rice is tender.

In a frypan, saute onion with shortening, remaining garlic and tomatoes. Add the meat and season with salt and pepper. When meat is cooked, add raisins and parsley.

Grease a baking dish. Make a layer of rice, then a layer of meat; repeat, then top with a layer of rice. Dot with shortening and place under a low broiler flame for 3 minutes. Turn out on a serving platter and top with grated cheese. Garnish with hard-boiled eggs. Serves 8.

VIETNAMESE FRIED RICE

2½ cups water
2 cups uncooked rice
3 eggs, slightly beaten
1 tsp. vegetable oil

1 bunch scallions,
  chopped
2 beef boullion cubes,
  or 2 tsp. beef extract

Add water to saucepan, bring to a boil and add beef bouillon. When dissolved, add rice and cook until all the water is absorbed. Stir two or three times to prevent sticking. Turn heat to low. Stir again after rice has cooked another 5 minutes. Cook until tender.

Cool the rice before frying.

Pour oil into a large heavy skillet and heat. Add rice and sauce for 7 minutes, stirring constantly. Add eggs and stir well. Cook another 5 minutes. Add chopped scallions and cook for 3–4 minutes more. Fried bacon may be added.

Serve hot, with soy sauce if desired. Serves 4.

CHOP CHAI

KOREA

½ lb. Chinese noodles
3 large carrots, sliced
    in very fine strips
4 medium dried onions,
    sliced
½ cup chopped parsley
½ lb. sirloin steak,
    sliced into 2-inch
    by ½-inch strips
½ cup celery, chopped
    and salted

6 green onions, cut
    into thin slivers
½ clove garlic, minced
2 tbs. soy sauce
2 tbs. white sesame
    seed, browned and
    pulverized
1 tsp. sugar
Pinch black pepper
Salt to taste
Sesame oil

Drop noodles into boiling water and cook 15 minutes. Drain, rinse in cold water, drain again and set aside.

Add 1 tbs. oil to a hot skillet, add carrots and fry, stirring constantly until barely cooked. Set aside.

Add additional oil to the skillet and fry sliced onions the same way. Set aside.

Wash salt from celery, drain and fry lightly in oil. Set aside.

Slightly wilt parsley in hot oil.

Fry steak strips in 1 tbs. oil along with the green onions, and minced garlic. Fry until steak is tender.

Combine all ingredients as follows. Place fried steak strips in a large bowl. Add the fried vegetables and noodles. Season with soy sauce, sesame seeds, sugar, black pepper and salt. Toss lightly, turn onto a large platter. Serves 4.

LIU MEIN

CHINA

1 lb. fine noodles	½ cup lichen
1 lb. meat strips of beef, pork, veal or lamb	1 cup celery in strips
1 tbs. cornstarch	1 cup cooked bamboo shoots
2 tbs. pork fat or butter	1 cup mushrooms
½ cup onions	1 cup string beans
2 cups bean sprouts	1 cup meat stock

In a large, heavy skillet fry meat in butter until lightly browned. Moisten meat strips first in soy sauce, then roll in cornstarch. Return to skillet and saute 5 minutes. Add the vegetables and mix well. Moisten with a little meat stock, cover and steam for 5 minutes longer. Set aside.

In boiling salted water, cook noodles 5 minutes. Drain.

In a greased baking pan, arrange a layer of noodles and a layer of meat mixture alternately, until all the noodles and meat mixture have been used. Top off with the meat mixture and bake 10 minutes in a moderate oven (400°F). Serve hot. Serves 6 to 8.

FRIED RICE WITH SHRIMPS

CHINA

1 lb. fresh shrimps or prawns	4 cups boiled rice
1 chopped large onion	1 stalk celery, chopped
½ cup halved mushrooms	3 tbs. soy sauce
3 tbs. vegetable oil	1 tsp. salt
	4 eggs

Wash shrimps and drop into salted boiling water for 10 minutes. Drain and allow to cool. Remove shells and devein.

In a large skillet, saute chopped onions, celery,

mushrooms and shrimps for 5 minutes in vegetable oil. Add rice, soy sauce and salt. Cook and stir until all ingredients are well mixed.

Beat eggs slightly and add. Stir in and continue cooking until eggs are well done. Serves 6.

MI XAO DON

VIETNAM

½ lb. fine noodles	1 clove garlic, crushed
¼ lb. cabbage, shredded	Dash black pepper
1 lb. celery, shredded	1 tbs. chopped onion
1½ lbs. ground pork	⅓ cup fish soy or ¼ cup soy sauce with ½ tsp. salt added
Sugar to taste	

In a bowl, combine the fish soy, sugar, garlic, pepper and onion. Mix well and stir until sugar is dissolved. If fish soy is not available and soy sauce is substituted, omit sugar. Add meat and mix well. Set aside.

Throw noodles into boiling water and cook 4-5 minutes, or until they bend but are not thoroughly cooked. Rinse in cold water and drain. When noodles are dry, fry until brown in deep fat (approximately 3-4 minutes).

Heat an oiled skillet. Fry meat until red color is gone. Add cabbage and then celery. Cook for 15 minutes. Serve hot on top of fried noodles. Salt to taste. Serves 3.

RICE MOMOTOMBO

NICARAGUA

1 cup rice	½ cup diced green pepper
2 tbs. butter	2 medium tomatoes, cut in cubes
2 cups hot water	1 tsp. salt
½ cup diced onion	

In a large frying pan, saute rice in butter until light brown.

Add water, pepper, onion, tomatoes and salt. Boil until water is absorbed and rice is tender. Cover and let steam until ready to serve.

Rice Momotombo may be served in several ways. It may be browned in the oven or baked with grated cheese. Garnish with parsley and red peppers.

It is especially delicious when served with an avocado salad and Canadian bacon. Serves 4 to 6.

PANCIT QUISADO

PHILIPPINES

½ cup boiled chicken, flaked
½ cup boiled shrimp, sliced
½ cup boiled pork, in strips
½ cup boiled ham, in strips
1 cup shredded cabbage
3 tbs. soy sauce
2 lbs. thin rice or egg noodles
4 cloves garlic
1 sliced medium onion
1 cup shrimp juice
1½ cups chicken stock
Lemon slices
Salt and pepper to taste
2 tbs. oil

In a large skillet fry *separately* the garlic, onion, shrimp, pork, chicken and ham. Set aside a portion of each dish for garnishing.

Return the remaining fried foods to the skillet. Add the soy sauce, shrimp juice, salt and pepper. Cook 5 minutes, then add cabbage and mix well. Simmer slowly until almost dry.

Blanch noodles in boiling water for about 2 minutes, then fry in oil. Add noodles to the meat mixture.

To serve, arrange on a platter and garnish with lemon slices and the garlic, meats and onion previously set aside. Serves 6.

TAMALE TIMBALES

GUATEMALA

1 small onion, minced
½ green pepper
¼ cup butter
12 oz. can whole kernel
  corn, drained and put
  through food grinder
1 cup yellow cornmeal
3 eggs, well beaten

2 cups tomato sauce
¾ cup cream
½ cup grated Parmesan
  cheese
1 tsp. chili powder
Salt to taste

Saute onion and green pepper gently in butter for 5 minutes. Add all remaining ingredients, mixing well.

Turn into 8 well-greased custard cups and set in a shallow pan of hot water. Bake in a moderate oven (375°F) about 40 minutes, or until firm. (Mixture may be baked in a 1½-quart ring mold for 50-60 minutes, if preferred.)

Remove from oven and let stand a few minutes before removing from mold. Serve with creamed chicken, to be spooned over the timbales. Serves 8.

PORK BALLS WITH SOTANGHON

CHINA

½ cup ground pork
2 tbs. chopped onion
1 tbs. flour
½ tbs. salt
¼ tbs. pepper
1 egg
2 cloves garlic, crushed
2 tbs. sliced onion

2 cups broth
½ cup sotanghon,
  soaked and cut (or
  egg noodles or
  vermicelli)
2 tbs. soy sauce
¼ cup green onions,
  chopped fine

Beat the egg slightly in a bowl and add the pork, onion, flour, salt and pepper. Knead and shape into balls about 1-inch in diameter.

In a skillet, saute the garlic in a little oil until light brown. Add the onion and cook until tender. Add the broth and bring to a boil. Drop the meatballs one by one into the boiling broth and cook until meat is done.

Add the noodles and continue cooking until the noodles are barely done. Add soy sauce.

Just before serving, sprinkle with green onion. Serves 6.

MEATBALLS WITH MISUA

PHILIPPINES

1 cup ground leftover meat
2 tbs. chopped onion
2 cloves garlic, minced
1 egg
1 tbs. lard or butter
2 tbs. flour
1 tbs. green onion, chopped

6 cups rice water
6 cups misua, or egg noodles cut in short lengths
Soy sauce to taste
Salt and pepper to taste

In a frypan, saute garlic and onion in butter. Add meat, green onion and egg, mixing well. Set aside to cool.

When slightly cooled, form meat mixture into meatballs ½-inch in diameter. Roll balls in flour.

To a skillet add rice water and boil. Drop meatballs one by one into boiling rice water and cook 5 minutes. Add egg noodles and cook until done. Season with soy sauce and pepper. Add chopped green onions, salt and pepper to boiling mixture. Serve hot. Serves 6.

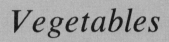

Vegetables

SIKIMICH'I KUK

KOREA

½ lb. fresh lean pork
¼ tsp. finely chopped
 garlic
4 tsp. sesame oil
2 lbs. fresh spinach
1½ tsp. salt

2 tbs. sesame seed,
 browned and pulverized
2 tbs. finely chopped
 green onion with tops
1 egg, beaten
Dash of black pepper

Discard tough stems and leaves from spinach. Wash and cut into 2-inch lengths.

Chop pork finely. Heat oil in kettle and brown pork with garlic, stirring constantly. Add spinach and salt. Cook slowly for 15 minutes or until spinach is tender, stirring occasionally. Add the green onion, sesame seed, black pepper and egg. Mix well and serve immediately. Serves 6.

KISAMVU

AFRICA

The combination of peanuts, onions and tomatoes that goes into many African dishes is intriguing. This sauce, without the cassava leaves, is used with almost any vegetable and is delicious.

½ cup peanuts, roasted
1 cup dried cassava
 leaves or spinach
1 medium onion,
 chopped
1 tomato, peeled and
 chopped

1 cup water
1 tbs. oil
Salt to taste
2 tbs. butter

Soak cassava or spinach leaves in water for 1 hour, then cook as you would spinach.

Remove the red skins from the peanuts, pound or grind them and mix with a little water to form a paste.

In a skillet, melt the butter and fry onions until golden. Add the tomato and peanut paste. Season to taste.

Drain the cassava leaves and add to the sauce. Mix well and cook 5 minutes longer. Serve with ugali, rice or boiled and mashed yams. Serves 4 to 6.

STUFFED SQUASH

CHINA

The Chinese, much like the people of the Near East, often use meat simply to give flavor to vegetables.

1 squash	½ cup sliced water
1½ cups chopped meat	chestnuts
(chicken, beef or	1 tbs. mushrooms
mixed)	½ cup water
2 tbs. soy sauce	

Remove seeds from the squash, slice and add remaining ingredients which have been thoroughly mixed.

Place ingredients in top half of a double boiler, add water and soy sauce and steam until well done. Serves 4.

BROCCOLI

CHINA

2 lbs. broccoli
½ lb. Chinese sausages

Skin the broccoli and cut into bite-sized pieces. Cook in hot vegetable oil until tender. Add sliced Chinese sausages and keep warm until served. Serves 6.

COCONUT TURON

PHILIPPINES

1 cup grated coconut
1½ cups boiled,
   mashed sweet
   potatoes

½ cup condensed milk
2 tbs. melted butter
Flavor with anise or
   vanilla to taste

Mix all ingredients together. Wrap about 2 tablespoons together in lumpia wrappers (page 57). Seal edge with water.
Fry in deep fat until brown and crisp. Serves 4.

CURRIED OKRA

AFRICA

Sister Patricia Hafey tells us that okra is called "lady fingers" in her part of Africa. When you see them, long and slender, it is easy to tell why.

12 or 14 okra, cut into
   short lengths
2 small chili peppers
1 cup chopped onion
1¼ tsp. coriander
1 tsp. tumeric
1 tsp. chili powder

1 tsp. curry powder
1 tsp. salt
Juice of 1 lemon
Milk from 1 coconut,
   diluted to 1½ cups
   with water
2 tbs. oil

Use canned okra if fresh is not available (2 cans). Saute okra in oil for several minutes. Add onions, chili pepper and curry powder. Remove from pan and set aside.
Heat coconut milk to boiling and pour over the grated coconut. Allow to cool, strain well and use this liquid to prepare sauce.
Use the same frying pan to make sauce. Add coconut liquid and the rest of the seasonings. Stir to mix well. Return the okra-onion mixture and simmer until thick. Serve with boiled rice. Serves 4 to 6.

PLANTAINS IN MOLE SAUCE

GUATEMALA

2 ripe cooking bananas,
  sliced
1 oz. sunflower seeds
Sesame seeds as
  needed
3 medium tomatoes

2 tbs. butter
1 chili pepper
1 stick cinnamon
1 sweet roll
½ oz. sweet chocolate
Salt to taste

Fry sliced bananas (plantain) in hot butter.

Toast and then grind together the sunflower seeds and sesame seeds.

Boil, then grind together tomatoes, pepper, cinnamon stick, chocolate and sweet roll. Fry mixture in butter.

Add fried bananas and simmer in sauce for a few minutes. Serve hot sprinkled with sesame seeds. Serves 4.

CHENGA

AFRICA

One of the daily tasks for girls is to pound enough dried corn for the day's requirements. This dish, usually made with this freshly ground corn, was sent to us by Sister Patricia Hafey.

1 cup cornmeal or
  coarsely pounded corn
½ cup corn flour

½ tsp. salt
½ cup thick sour cream

Soak the coarsely ground corn or cornmeal overnight. Then cook together with salt until soft. Thicken with the corn flour which has been mixed with a little water.

Cook mixture for about 15 minutes, remove from the heat and add the sour cream.

Set aside to cool, then chill. This dish is served cold. Serves 6.

SQUASH WITH COCONUT

PHILIPPINES

2 cups squash, cubed
1 cup thick coconut
    milk
½ cup shrimp stock
½ cup shrimp, chopped

½ sliced medium onion
2 cloves garlic, sliced
1 tsp. butter or lard
Salt to taste

Saute the garlic, onion and shrimp in butter or lard. Add shrimp stock and stir until it comes to a boil. Add squash and cook until done. Season with salt.

Just before removing from heat, add thick coconut milk and continue to simmer for 2 minutes. Serve hot. Serves 4.

SWEET POTATO CURRY

AFRICA

2 cups sweet potatoes
    or yams
3 cups sliced yellow
    squash or pumpkin
1 tbs. butter
2 cups tomatoes,
    chopped

¾ cup chopped onion
1 tsp. curry powder
⅔ cup peanuts
Salt to taste

Peel and slice together the potatoes and the pumpkin or squash, then cook in boiling water until just tender.

Fry onions in butter until golden, add tomatoes and simmer for about 10 minutes.

Boil salted peanuts in a little salted water, then shell and remove jackets. Mash the peanuts and add to the tomato sauce. Add the seasonings and then the parboiled potatoes and pumpkin. Simmer for 20 minutes, adding water as needed.

Africans like this curry well mashed and often serve it with a meat or stew. Serves 6–8.

CH'ENT'AI K'ONGIA SAI O POKKIM

KOREA

1¼ lbs. sliced green
  beans
½ cup fresh or canned
  shrimp
¼ cup soy sauce
1¼ tsp. sugar
2 tsp. white sesame
  seed, browned and
  pulverized

½ medium onion, sliced
  thin
3 tbs. sesame or
  salad oil

Wash and devein shrimp. Drain and cut into small pieces.

In a skillet, saute shrimp with onion in hot oil.

Wash beans and cut into diagonal pieces. Add beans, sugar and soy sauce to the shrimp and let mixture simmer until beans are cooked through, but still crisp. Serve hot. Serves 6.

EGGPLANT CASSEROLE

EGYPT

1 medium onion,
  chopped
¼ cup butter
1 lb. ground beef
½ cup tomato sauce

½ cup water
1 tsp. salt
Dash of pepper
1 medium eggplant

Melt 2 tbs. butter in the bottom of a saucepan. Add onions and saute until golden. Add beef and cook until brown.

Combine tomato sauce, water, pepper, salt and pour over meat mixture. Bring to a boil and cook for 5 minutes.

Remove mixture from heat. With a perforated spoon, remove meat from sauce.

Slice eggplant and brown lightly in remaining butter.

In a casserole, place alternating layers of eggplant and meat until all have been used. Pour sauce over the casserole and bake in a moderate oven for 25 minutes. Serves 6.

STRING BEANS

URUGUAY

1½ lbs. string beans	*3 tbs. butter*
1 tsp. salt	*1 tbs. minced parsley*
¼ tsp. pepper	*2 tbs. lemon juice*

Wash string beans and break into small pieces. Boil briskly in salted water in uncovered pan until beans are tender. Rinse in cold water.

Put beans in frying pan with butter, pepper and parsley. Cook for 10 minutes over high heat. Sprinkle with lemon juice just before serving. Serves 6 to 8.

GREEN OR WAX BEANS

CHINA

1 lb. beans	*½ cup soy sauce*
1 lb. pork	*3 tsp. butter or lard*
1 tsp. minced ginger root	*Salt to taste*
1 tsp. minced onion	

Cut pork into small cubes and fry in butter together with the minced ginger.

Add beans which have been cut into small pieces, onions and a little water or meat stock. Cook covered until tender. Serves 4 to 6.

PEKING ASPARAGUS

CHINA

¼ cup chicken stock
¼ cup water
2 tbs. sherry
2 tbs. soy sauce

1 tbs. cornstarch
1 large can (1 lb.)
  asparagus

Heat a pan, adding chicken stock, water sherry, soy sauce and cornstarch. Stir constantly until it begins to boil. Add asparagus and simmer until ready to serve. Serves 6.

PEPPY POTATOES

AFRICA

The variety of spices in this recipe make it a very tangy dish. If you'd prefer, try it using less spice, especially the chili powder and ginger.

3 cups raw potatoes,
  cubed or sliced
1½ cups tomatoes,
  cubed or sliced
¾ cup onions, chopped
1-inch piece ginger
  root sliced thin
2 tsp. parsley, chopped
  finely
2 tbs. oil
1 tsp. salt
½ cup water

Spice grind
1 pod cardamom
½ tsp. cummin seed
½-inch piece cinnamon
  bark
½ tsp. coriander seed
2 cloves
3 peppercorns
½ tsp. tumeric
⅛ tsp. chili powder

Grind together all the spices and set aside.
Saute the chopped onion and sliced ginger in a little oil. Add the ground spices and mix well. Add the potatoes and fry a few minutes longer until they are well coated with the spices. Add the tomatoes and parsley.

Add the water and sprinkle with salt. Cover the pan and simmer until potatoes are tender. Serve with a meat dish. Serves 4 to 6.

STUFFED EGGPLANT

ARABIA

½ cup olive oil
3 medium eggplants,
   halved
2 lbs. ground lamb

2 tsp. salt
1 tsp. pepper
1 cup tomato sauce
1 cup water

Place unpeeled eggplant in skillet to which 3 tbs. olive oil have been added. Fry 5 minutes on cut side, then 10 minutes on skin side.

In another skillet, heat remaining oil and add lamb, salt and pepper. Saute for 10 minutes. Place eggplants in casserole. Make pockets lengthwise in several places and stuff with lamb. Combine tomato sauce and water and pour over eggplant. Bake in 350° oven for 1 hour. Serves 6.

STUFFED MUSHROOMS

CHINA

1 cup minced chicken,
   pork, lamb or beef
½ cup minced ham
1 tbs. minced onion

6 large dried mush-
   rooms (or fresh)
1 tsp. soy sauce

Mix meats and onion and moisten with soy sauce.

Turn mushrooms upside down and remove stems. Stuff with mixture and steam in a steamer for about ½-hour. If dried mushrooms are used they should be soaked first in cold water.

Makes an excellent entree or luncheon dish. Serves 6.

LENTILS

AFRICA

1 cup yellow lentils   ½ cup onion, chopped
1 cup raw rice   Salt to taste
1 cup coconut milk

Soak lentils overnight and then slip them out of their skins. In a large saucepan, cover the lentils with water and cook.

Wash and cook the rice in 1 cup water.

Saute the chopped onion in a small amount of oil until golden.

Prepare 1 cup coconut milk by pouring 1 cup boiling water over 1 cup of grated coconut. Allow to stand until cool, then strain.

When rice and lentils are almost cooked, add them to the fried onions in the skillet and add the coconut milk. Season with a little salt. Simmer until some of the liquid has evaporated, stirring occasionally.

This can be served with a meat or fish dish. Serves 6.

QUICOY

GUATEMALA

6 large quicoy or   2 medium tomatoes,
   medium zucchini   cut fine
4 strips bacon, minced   1 tbs. chopped parsley
1 medium onion,   Salt and pepper to taste
   minced

Saute minced bacon and onion until tender. Add parsley, quicoy cut in rounds about ½-inch thick, tomatoes, salt and pepper. *Do not use any water.*

Allow to cook over a slow heat until tender, stirring occasionally. Serves 3.

AMPALAYA VEGETABLE

PHILIPPINES

3 tbs. cooking oil
1 tsp. crushed garlic
2 tbs. sliced onion
¼ cup sliced tomato
1 cup boiled pork, diced
⅓ cup shrimp, peeled
   and cut lengthwise
2 cups shrimp stock
2 cups rice water
   (first washing)

2 tsp. salt
Dash of pepper
1 cup sotanghon (rice
   noodles, or egg
   noodles)
2 cups ampalaya,
   sliced or acorn
   squash

Saute the garlic to a light brown and add onion. Cook for 2 minutes. Add tomatoes, pork and shrimp. Cook for 3 minutes and add shrimp stock and rice water. Cover and bring to a boil. Add salt and pepper, and if desired, 1 tsp. soy sauce. Add noodles and cook for 5 minutes. Add ampalaya, cover and cook 5 minutes longer.

Serve hot with boiled rice. Bananas make a good dessert for this meal. Serves 8.

STUFFED CABBAGE LEAVES

SAUDI ARABIA

1 cup raw rice
½ lb. ground lamb
½ cup butter
1 tsp. salt

½ tsp. cinnamon
1 small head cabbage
2 cups tomato juice

Cook rice in water until tender. Drain and place in a large mixing bowl. Add meat, butter and seasonings. Form mixture into small rolls.

Cook individual cabbage leaves in small amount of water for 5 minutes. Drain and dry. Wrap cabbage leaves around meat rolls and lay in a heavy skillet. Add tomato juice, cover and cook for ½ hour over medium heat. Serves 6.

HOT K'ONG NAMUL

KOREA

4 cups canned bean
  sprouts
1½ finely chopped
  green onion with tops
1 tsp. soy sauce
1 tbs. white sesame
  seed, browned and
  pulverized

¼ tsp. salt
Pinch cayenne pepper
1 tbs. sesame or
  salad oil

Drain bean sprouts.

In a skillet, heat the oil, add bean sprouts and salt. Saute only long enough to thoroughly heat the vegetable. If fresh bean sprouts are used, fry 15 minutes. Add other seasonings and serve hot. Serves 4.

SWEET POTATO BALLS

CHINA

½ lb. shredded coconut
1 cup chopped almonds
2 tsp. butter
1 cup sugar

½ lb. mashed sweet
  potatoes
1 lb. rice flour or
  other flour

Mix shredded coconut and nuts with sugar and butter, and steam until butter melts.

Mix mashed sweet potatoes and flour into a paste. Roll out thin on board and cut into circles about 2½-inches in diameter.

Fill with coconut filling and shape into small balls.

Fry in deep fat until golden brown, drain and serve. Serves 6.

CUCUMBERS

CHINA

4 large cucumbers	1 tsp. cornstarch
1 cup chicken broth	1 cup shredded ham

Peel and remove seeds from cucumbers. Cut into wedges. Boil in plain water until tender. Drain and wash in cold water.

In a frypan, place cucumbers, chicken broth and heat. Gradually add cornstarch and cook until slightly thickened.

Serve topped with shredded ham. Serves 4.

UGALI MADE WITH BEANS

AFRICA

Sister Margaret Hart tells us there are various kinds of ugali, a sort of "mush" usually made of freshly ground dried corn boiled with water. This version is made with beans and peanuts.

2 cups dried beans, any kind	2 cups boiling water or liquid from the beans
3 tbs. roasted peanuts	1 medium chopped onion
2 tbs. oil	
2 tbs. flour	

Soak the beans until the skins can be removed easily. Remove the skins from the roasted peanuts. Boil beans and peanuts together until well cooked, then drain and puree the mixture, reserving the liquid.

Fry the onion in oil until golden. Slowly add the flour stirring constantly with a fork. When the flour is slightly browned, add the hot liquid from the beans and stir until it makes a gravy-like substance. Do not let it thicken too much.

Add the mashed beans and peanuts and cook for a few minutes. Salt to taste. The resulting dish should be of the consistency of a cornmeal mush. Serve with hot meat or vegetables in gravy. Serves 4 to 6.

CARAMELIZED SWEET POTATOES

CHINA

1 lb. sweet potatoes	2 cups brown sugar
2 eggs	1 cup water
½ tsp. salt	
2 tbs. bean or other flour	

Wash and peel sweet potatoes. Grate into a bowl, add salt and the slightly beaten eggs. Add flour and mix well.

Drop mixture by spoonfuls into deep boiling fat. Fry to a golden brown. Drain and serve with a thick syrup made from brown sugar and water. Serves 4.

STRING BEANS

GUATEMALA

Cracker crumbs, as needed	1 medium minced onion
1 lb. string beans	1 cup tomatoes, peeled and diced
3 eggs, beaten	1 minced chili pepper
1 tbs. butter	

Prepare a weak batter from eggs and cracker crumbs. Cook string beans in salted water, drain and dry.

Dip bunches of cooked beans in the batter and fry in deep fat until golden. Drain.

In a skillet, saute together butter, onions and minced chili pepper. Add tomatoes, cover and simmer for ½ hour.

To serve, cover beans with tomato sauce. Season with salt and pepper. Serves 4.

POROTOS GRANADOS

CHILE

1 cup corn niblets or
  niblets from 4 ears of
  fresh corn
½ lb. yellow squash,
  cubed

2 lbs. beans
1 medium onion,
  chopped
2 tbs. butter or lard

Cook beans in enough boiling water so that some liquid remains.

In a skillet, saute onions in butter until golden. Add fried onions together with the corn and squash to the beans about ½ hour before beans are done. Simmer all ingredients together for remaining time. Serves 6.

BAMBOO SHOOTS

CHINA

3 cups bamboo shoots
1 cup Chinese mush-
  rooms
3 cups flour

Water as needed
Soy sauce to taste
Sesame oil to taste
Wheat flour as needed

Steam bamboo shoots until tender. Add mushrooms and keep hot. Garnish with wheat strings made as follows (or egg noodles).

Make a ball of wheat flour and cold water. Knead it in the hand until it is firm. Now hold ball under cold running water until only strings remain. Place these strings on top of bamboo shoots. Continue until shoots are well garnished. As this is a very difficult process, many Chinese prefer to garnish with egg noodles.

Add soy sauce to taste and top with a bit of sesame oil. Serves 6.

Fruits, Desserts, and Candies

APPLE DELIGHT

IRAN

4 medium apples
2 tbs. lemon juice
6 tbs. powdered sugar

2 tsp. rosewater
4 ice cubes

Pare and grate apples, sprinkling immediately with lemon juice to prevent darkening. Add sugar and rosewater. Stir. Add ice cubes to chill and dilute mixture. Serve in individual dishes. Serves 4.

TORTA CON PIÑA

CHILE

Sister Genevieve Reinhardt says that this cake is a delectable treat for fiestas, birthdays, anniversaries or any time the Chilean family wants a special dessert.

12 eggs, separated
6 tbs. potato flour
6 tbs. wheat flour
12 tbs. sugar
3 tbs. baking powder
2 cans crushed
   pineapple

½ lb. butter
2 tbs. powdered sugar
1 tsp. powdered instant
   coffee
1 pint heavy cream,
   chilled

In a mixing bowl beat egg whites until they stand in peaks. Add sugar by spoonfuls and continue beating. Add egg yolks, one by one, beating the while. Add the sifted dry ingredients, a little at a time, folding in gently. Pour into well-greased baking pan and bake at 375°F for 20 minutes or until done. Cool, remove from pan and cut each cake into 2 layers.

While the cake is baking, cream the butter and 2 tbs. powdered sugar. When the cake has cooled, spread butter mixture on each layer. Over that spread the drained pineapple, which may be drizzled with a bit of the pineapple juice to keep cake moist. Assemble the layers as for any layer cake.

Pour the heavy cream into an iced mixing bowl. Add sugar to taste and the powdered instant coffee. Whip until stiff. Frost cake with whipped cream.

LUAU SPONGE CAKE

HAWAII

1¼ cups sifted cake
   flour
¼ cup sugar
¼ tsp. salt
5 egg whites
1 tsp. cream of tartar

¼ cup sugar
¾ cup light corn syrup
5 egg yolks
½ tsp. vanilla
½ tsp. lemon extract

Mix and sift flour, sugar and salt. Sift twice more. Add cream of tartar to egg whites and beat until mixture slightly mounds when beater is raised. Beat in sugar. Blend in corn syrup and continue beating until whites stand in firm peaks. Beat egg yolks until thick, then beat in vanilla and lemon extract. Fold egg yolks into egg-white mixture. Gradually fold in dry ingredients, sifting about ¼ cup at a time over the surface. Pour batter into ungreased 10x4-inch tube pan. Cut through with knife to remove air spaces. Bake in slow (325°) oven for 50 minutes or until cake springs back lightly when touched with fingers. Invert pan and cool 1 hour before removing. Cover with favorite egg-white frosting over which is sprinkled shredded coconut, toasted light brown.

SESAME SEED LEAVES

CHINA

⅓ cup egg whites
⅔ cup water
Flour, as needed

Sesame seeds, as
   needed
Salt to taste

Add egg whites to water and beat slightly. Begin adding flour, enough to make a stiff dough.

On a floured board, roll dough out thin. Scatter sesame seeds on it and sprinkle with salt. Roll seeds and salt firmly into the surface.

Cut dough into oblongs, 2½ by 4 inches. Slash in the center.

Fry in deep fat, drain and serve.

BANANA TART

BRAZIL

4 large bananas
½ cup sugar
⅛ tsp. salt
1 tbs. butter
¼ cup white wine

½ tsp. nutmeg
1 baked pastry shell, or
   individual pastry
   shells
Whipping cream

Peel bananas and press through a sieve. Put pulp into a saucepan and add sugar, salt and butter. Cook mixture until it starts to boil, stirring meanwhile. Allow to cool, then whip in wine and nutmeg. Pour into pastry shell, top with whipped cream. The juice of one lime may be substituted for the wine. Also, a firmer mixture can be obtained by adding a teaspoon of plain gelatin as mixture cools. Serves 4 to 6.

CARAMEL CUSTARD

PHILIPPINES

1 pint coffee
1 pint cream
12 egg yolks
5 tbs. sugar

Grated rind ½ lime
Juice of one lime
1 cup sugar

Mix coffee and cream, scald in top of double boiler. Beat egg yolks and sugar together. Pour coffee cream over egg mixture, stirring. Add lime rind and juice. Melt (caramelize) the cup of sugar and use to coat 2-quart baking dish. Pour in cream mixture. Set dish in pan of hot water. Bake at 350° in oven about 1 hour, or until silver knife inserted in center is clean. Serve ice cold. Serves 8 to 10.

SPICE CAKE

LIBERIA

⅔ cup butter
¾ cup sugar
4 eggs
2¼ cups flour
¾ tsp. soda
½ tsp. cinnamon
½ tsp. allspice
¼ tsp. mace
½ tsp. baking powder

⅛ tsp. cloves
⅔ cup light molasses
½ cup milk
⅓ cup citron, cut very fine
½ cup seedless raisins, chopped
½ cup shredded coconut

Heat oven to 350°. Cream butter and sugar. Add eggs, one at a time. Sift together dry ingredients and stir in alternately with mixture of milk and molasses. Stir until smooth. Fold in fruit and coconut. Pour batter into 2 greased and floured loaf pans, approximately 9x5x2½ inches. Bake 35 to 40 minutes.

TORTA HELADA

PERU OR BOLIVIA

This very special cake is baked in Arequipa for very festive occasions, such as a wedding or anniversary. It takes some time to prepare and usually is made a day or two before it will be served.

8 eggs, separated
1½ cups flour
1½ cups sugar
½ cup cornstarch
2 tsp. baking powder

Gelatin layer
2 pkgs. lemon gelatin
  dessert
Water, as needed
1 can sliced pineapple
1 bottle maraschino
  cherries

Filling
1 can evaporated milk
  well chilled
2 cups orange juice
2 envelopes unflavored
  gelatin
1½ cups sugar

Beat egg whites until they stand in stiff peaks. Add the egg yolks, one by one, and continue beating until the mass is light and fluffy. Add the sugar, a little at a time, beating all the while. Sift together the flour and cornstarch and fold into the egg mixture. Do not beat.

Pour batter into well greased pan and bake at 350°F until done. Remove from pan and allow to cook. Slice into 3 layers.

After the cake has been removed from its baking pan, prepare lemon layer. Make a lemon gelatin dessert according to the recipe on the package, but omit ½ cup of water. Pour half the mixture into the same cake pan in which the cake was baked. Allow to set. When gelatin layer is set, cover with a layer of pineapple slices and cherries and pour in the remainder of the lemon gelatin dessert. Allow to set. Then chill overnight in the refrigerator.

The day the cake is to be served, dissolve the unflavored gelatin in ½ cup hot water after moistening with a little orange juice.

In a bowl, beat the evaporated milk until thick and stiff. Mix the gelatin with the rest of the orange juice and add to the whipped milk. Mix thoroughly.

This "upside-down" cake is assembled in the same pan in which it was baked, now containing the lemon gelatin, fruit mixture. To assemble, place the top layer of cake on top of the chilled lemon gelatin. Cover this with a layer of the whipped milk-orange juice mixture. Add the center layer of cake, then another layer of the whipped milk mixture. Cover with the bottom layer of cake, browned side up. A little pineapple juice may be sprinkled over each layer. Place this in the refrigerator to chill thoroughly, at least 4 hours.

To remove cake from pan, place pan in ½-inch of hot water for several minutes. Cover pan with serving dish and invert quickly. Cake will drop out with gelatin layer on top. Frost sides with sweetened whipped cream, leaving the lemon gelatin-fruit layer exposed. The result is beautiful as well as delicious and well worth the time and effort. Serves 12 to 16.

BANANAS IN RUM

HAITI

6 large, ripe bananas	3 tbs. rum
½ cup olive oil	¼ cup powdered sugar
½ tsp. vanilla	

Peel bananas and cut across in thin slices. Fry in hot olive oil. (Another cooking oil may be substituted if desired.) As soon as bananas are browned slightly, remove from oil, cool and drain on brown paper. Place in shallow serving dish. Add vanilla to rum and sprinkle mixture over the bananas. Sieve the powdered sugar over the top. Put in refrigerator to chill. Serve ice cold. Serves 6.

FLOUR PUDDING

NEPAL

½ lb. sweet butter,
    unsalted
2 cups cake flour
6 tbs. sugar

6 tbs. raisins, chopped
6 tbs. chopped almonds
Pinch saffron

Mix flour and sugar. Melt butter in heavy saucepan. Stir flour and sugar mixture into butter, adding raisins and almonds. Cook over low heat, stirring constantly until flour is golden brown. Add saffron. Let mixture cool until it can be handled. Knead and form into a roll about 2 inches in diameter (similar to an icebox cookie roll). Cover slices with your favorite custard sauce. Serves 6.

RICE DOUGHNUTS

AFRICA

More and more stores now carry at least one variety of rice flour. In Africa, however, young girls make it by pounding or grinding rice that has dried out a bit after having soaked in water overnight.

1 cup grated coconut
4 cups rice flour
2½ tsp. baking powder

1 tsp. cinnamon
1 cup sugar
1 cup boiling water

Make coconut milk by pouring boiling water over the grated coconut. Allow it to stand until cool, then strain and squeeze the pulp.

In a bowl sift together the flour, sugar, baking powder and cinnamon. Mix in the cooled coconut milk and beat until it is smooth and elastic and bubbles begin to form. Cover with a loose cloth and allow to raise overnight in a cool place.

The following day, drop by spoonfuls into deep, hot oil. Fry until golden brown, turning only once. Drain and serve hot.

GUAVA SHERBET

HAWAII

2½ cups canned
  guava juice
2 tbs. lemon juice
⅔ cup whipped cream

1 cup sugar
2 egg whites, stiffly
  beaten
Pinch of salt

In a saucepan, cook sugar and juice slowly for 10 minutes. Add the lemon juice, stir, cool and pour into a refrigerator freezing tray. Allow to freeze firm, then remove the mixture to an iced mixing bowl. Beat with a rotary egg beater until light. Add whipped cream and fold in stiffly beaten egg whites to which the salt has been added. Pour into the freezer tray and refreeze. Serve ice cold. Serves 8.

MARGOD

AFGHANISTAN

½ cup sugar
1¾ cups water or milk
⅛ tsp. salt
¼ cup cornstarch

½ cup water or milk
½ cup pistachio nuts,
  chopped

Mix sugar and salt into the water or milk and bring mixture to a boil in a double boiler. Meanwhile mix cornstarch and the ½ cup of water or milk, stirring until smooth. Gradually add cornstarch mixture to boiling mixture, stirring constantly. Cook the pudding over boiling water for 20 minutes, or cook and stir over very low heat until pudding thickens and loses raw-cornstarch taste. Cool and pour into a wet mold. Chill. Sprinkle serving with pistachio nuts. Serves 6.

ALMOND CAKES

CHINA

1 lb. flour	¼ tsp. salt dissolved
½ lb. butter	in 1 tsp. water
½ lb. sugar	1 cup roasted almonds
5 eggs, beaten	

In a mixing bowl, cream butter with sugar. Add eggs, salt water and mix well. Add flour and make a smooth paste.

Roll out on a floured board into a thin sheet, about ¼-inch thick. Cut sheet into 1½-inch round cakes, placing a whole roasted almond in the center of each one.

Fry in sesame oil, drain and serve. Makes about 40 cakes.

MANGO CREAM PIE

HAWAII

5 or 6 mangoes	4 tbs. sugar
2 tbs. flour	½ cup sugar
Baked pie shell	2 eggs, separated

Peel and slice mangoes and cook together with ½ cup sugar until tender.

Beat egg yolks until golden. Add flour and mix thoroughly. Add flour-egg mixture to mangoes, bring to a boil and cook 2 more minutes to thicken.

Pour mixture into pastry shell and cover with meringue made from egg whites beaten with 4 tbs. sugar.

Bake in a 300° oven until meringue is browned.

COCOA CAKES

COLOMBIA

¼ *pound butter*
  (or shortening)
1½ *cups sugar*
3 *eggs*
¾ *cup cocoa powder*

1½ *cups flour, sifted*
3 *tsp. baking powder*
⅔ *cup milk*
1 *tsp. vanilla extract*

Cream butter until it is soft and add the sugar gradually. Beat until fluffy. Add the eggs, beating well. Sift the cocoa, flour and baking powder together, blend in butter and sugar mixture alternately with the milk. Add the vanilla and mix well. Grease 2 cupcake tins lightly and dust them with flour. Fill the pans two-thirds full with mixture and bake in a preheated oven at 350°F for 20 minutes. Cocoa cakes may be served hot or cold. Makes 16 cakes.

VERMICELLI PUDDING

PAKISTAN

1 *tsp. saffron*
1 *tsp. water*
¼ *cup shredded*
  almonds
¼ *cup pistachio nuts*
½ *cup seedless raisins*
½ *pound (1 cup) butter*
2 *cardamom seeds*

2 *3-inch sticks*
  cinnamon
½ *pound (3½ cups)*
  vermicelli
2 *tall cans evaporated*
  milk
2 *cups sugar*

Melt butter with spices. Add raw vermicelli; cook slowly 5 minutes. Add milk; cook slowly until milk is absorbed and vermicelli tender (about 20 minutes). Remove cardamom seeds and cinnamon. Stir in sugar. Mix saffron with water and add to mixture. Stir in nuts and raisins. Cover, let stand 5 minutes. Serve warm. Makes 5 good cups (generous servings).

CORNSTARCH CAKE

EGYPT

1 cup eggs (4 or 5 eggs)	2 cups sifted cornstarch
1 cup sifted, powdered sugar	1 tsp. vanilla
1 cup butter or margarine	½ tsp. baking powder
	¼ to ½ cup powdered sugar

Beat eggs thoroughly, then beat in cup of powdered sugar and blend in butter. Continue beating, gradually adding cornstarch. Beat in vanilla and baking powder. Bake in greased 8x8x2-inch pan at 375° for 25 to 30 minutes. Sprinkle with powdered sugar as soon as taken from oven.

CARAMEL SQUARES

CHINA

½ cup shortening	¾ cup walnuts, finely chopped
½ cup sugar	
3 egg yolks	Topping
1 egg white	2 egg whites
1 tsp. vanilla	1¾ cups light brown sugar
1 cup flour	½ tsp. vanilla
1 tsp. baking powder	
¼ tsp. salt	
3 tbs. milk	

Blend the shortening and the sugar. Add egg yolks, egg white and beat well. To this add the vanilla, flour (which has been sifted with the baking powder), salt and milk. Spread mixture on well-greased baking pan and sprinkle with chopped walnuts. Over the chopped walnuts, this mixture may be spread:

Beat egg whites until stiff. Add sugar and vanilla and spread mixture over walnuts in pan. Bake about 30 minutes in medium oven (350°F). Cut in squares while warm. Makes 15 squares.

BAKED BANANA PUDDING

AFRICA

1 fresh coconut, grated	Water, as needed
1 cup coconut milk	2 bananas mashed
1 tbs. sugar	6 eggs, beaten

Grate the coconut meat. Add enough water to the coconut milk to make 1 cup of liquid. Heat the liquid to boiling and pour over grated coconut. Allow to cool. Strain and squeeze pulp.

Mash the bananas and fold them into the well beaten eggs. Add sugar. Pour in the coconut liquid, mixing well. Then add the grated coconut. Mix thoroughly.

Pour into a greased oven dish and bake at 325°F oven until mixture sets and is brown on top. Serve hot or cold. Serves 6.

PUMPKIN PUDDING

LAOS

1 whole pumpkin	5 eggs
(about 3 pounds)	6 tbs. sugar
2 cups boiling water	
1 cup freshly grated	
coconut	

Select a firm pumpkin with flat bottom that will stand with stem up. Cut off enough of stem end to form a lid and facilitate serving from pumpkin. Scrape out, discard seeds and fibrous flesh. Cover coconut with boiling water and let stand 20 minutes. Mix well and squeeze through cloth or fine sieve to make coconut milk. Beat eggs and add sugar. Mix into coconut milk. Pour whole into pumpkin and replace lid. Place pumpkin on rack in pot or kettle that can be tightly covered. Add water to pot to reach just below pumpkin. Steam until custard sets and pumpkin is tender. (Pudding may also be baked 1 hour at 350°.) Cool in refrigerator. Serve from pumpkin, spooning out both custard and pumpkin. Serves 4 to 6.

NUÉGADOS

GUATEMALA

Zilda Arevalo made these frosted cookies for a school party at Monte Maria. They were so delicious that the Sisters there asked for the recipe to share with friends.

1 lb. sifted flour	*Frosting*
2 tbs. baking powder	*1½ lbs. sugar*
2 eggs	*1½ cups water*
8 egg yolks	*1 egg white, beaten*
2 tbs. orange juice	
4 tbs. lukewarm water	

Sift together the flour and baking powder.

In another bowl beat together the eggs and egg yolks. Add orange juice and warm water. Then add the mixture to the flour, knead well and set aside for 1 hour.

Form dough into a rope about ¾-inch in diameter. Cut into small "fingers" about 2½-inches long. Then slice lengthwise in half.

Fry in deep fat until golden yellow.

Boil the sugar and water until it forms a thread. Pour slowly over the beaten egg white. Continue beating until it holds its shape.

Stir in the *nuégados* and coat them well.

Remove from the frosting, arrange in threes on waxed paper and allow to set. Makes 2-2½ lbs. cookies.

CARAMEL CUSTARD

MEXICO

6 egg yolks
4 cups milk
½ cup sugar
½ cup sifted flour

¼ tsp. salt
1 tsp. vanilla
½ cup light brown sugar

Beat the egg yolks slightly and set aside. Scald 3 cups of milk in top of double boiler. Mix sugar, flour and salt. Then stir in 1 cup of cold milk and the egg yolks. Now add mixture to scalded milk.

Continue cooking over boiling water, stirring constantly until thick. Remove from heat, let stand a few minutes and add the vanilla. Pour the custard into six pyrex serving dishes. When cold, sprinkle brown sugar over the top of each serving (generously).

Place baking dishes under broiler until the sugar caramelizes on top of each. Do not allow flame to touch top or sides of dishes. Place in refrigerator for several hours Serves 6.

Index by Countries